FACT AND RELEVANCE

ESSAYS ON HISTORICAL METHOD

Fact and Relevance

ESSAYS ON HISTORICAL METHOD

M. M. POSTAN

CAMBRIDGE

AT THE UNIVERSITY PRESS

1971

Published by the Syndics of the Cambridge University Press
Bentley House, 200 Euston Road, London N.W.1
American Branch: 32 East 57th Street, New York, N.Y.10022

ISBN: 0 521 07841 5

Printed in Great Britain
at the University Printing House, Cambridge
(Brooke Crutchley, University Printer)

CONTENTS

v

ACKNOWLEDGMENTS

Thanks are due to the following publishers and journals for permission to reproduce material first published by them (the essays concerned are indicated in brackets): *The Cambridge Journal* (1); *Sociological Review* (2 and 12); *Economic History Review* (4 and 7); *Historical Studies* (5); *Times Literary Supplement* (6); *Encounter* (8 and 9); Messrs Mouton (10); *Kölner Vorträge zur Sozial- und Wirtschaftsgeschichte* (11); Nicholson and Watson (13); and Thames and Hudson (14).

PREFACE

My decision to re-publish the essays in this book requires an explanation, perhaps even an apology. The essays have been selected and brought together on the strength of their common theme, which is that of the inter-relation of history and the social sciences. Indeed, the object of the publication is not to salvage a number of articles and lectures from oblivion, but to re-assert anew their point of view. In *anno domini* 1970 this re-assertion may turn out to be, to say the least, unpopular. Readers familiar with current intellectual fashions will find it only too easy to recognize and to docket this collection as 'positivist' or 'scientistic', and there is no need for me to remind them of the opprobrium which these dockets nowadays carry. Except for Marxists, most historians writing about the philosophy of history, most philosophers concerned with the methodology of historical and social study, and even some influential social anthropologists, have in recent years ranged themselves against the supposed fallacies of 'scientism'. They accept, however unconsciously, the idealistic dichotomy of 'physical' and 'humanistic' studies, or that of pure and practical reason, and consequently decry all attempts to use the methods of natural sciences in the study of history or of human affairs in general. It matters not that 'positivist' and 'scientistic' assumptions in fact underlie, as they must do, all current work of historical and socio-logical discovery. So unconscious is the average social scientist or historian of the gnoseological presuppositions of his study that he finds it only too easy to avow allegiance to doctrines wholly at variance with the philo-sophical pre-requisites of his own researches. Unfortunately, intellectual fashions are made up of avowed philosophies and not of assumed ones; and among avowed philosophies that represented by these essays ranks low.

However, to me the low ranking of my theme in philosophical fashions is merely an added justification for the decision to re-assert it. Nor am I, as a non-Marxist, deterred by the fact that Marxists now appear to be the sole protagonists of a point of view similar to mine, for I do not think it would be right to leave the Marxists in sole possession of the truth. All students of history and sociology must be reminded that they share with the Marxists a common descent from the scientific tradition and the scientific hope of the nineteenth century.

Such unity as these essays possess derives from their common theme:

otherwise they differ in the manner and the detail of their argument. Some were composed as deliberate attempts to state a methodological theory; others were forged in the heat of controversy; others still were conceived somewhat lightheartedly with the clear intention to provoke and even to irritate, and therefore present their case in an extreme, perhaps even paradoxical, form. Moreover, while some of the essays serve their common theme directly, others relate to it obliquely.

For all these reasons the essays are not arranged in the chronological order of their publication, but in that of their relevance. The three opening essays contain direct and more or less comprehensive statements of their point of view: the Germans would have called them 'programmatic'. The fourth and the fifth essays deal with two principal items of the programme – that of time sequences and that of theoretical relevances. The third group of the essays is made up of articles and lectures which in some way or other exemplify my general attitude to history and social sciences. Thus the two essays on macro-economics (numbers eight and nine) bring up to date, and to this extent correct, the references to economics in my inaugural lecture of 1938. Essays six, seven, eleven and twelve re-capitulate the general point of view with special reference to economic history in general or to individual topics of economic history. Least relevant may appear to be essays thirteen and fourteen. The reason why I have decided to include them is that the former may supplement and perhaps moderate my treatment of Marx and the Marxists in essay number three; while the latter may help to reconstruct the intellectual climate and the company in which the point of view represented by my essays was formed.

In preparing the essays for re-publication I refrained as far as I could from changing their original text. A few grammatical and stylistic emendations have, however, proved necessary. In essay number one several passages had to be slightly altered to make the essay as a whole intelligible without reference to Michael Oakeshott's article which had prompted it. Its title has been altered for the same reason. But in general the essays are now reproduced in their original version.

The decision to adhere to the original version may account for some of the statements to which I no longer subscribe. The earliest of the essays saw the light of day more than thirty years ago; and after a lapse of time as long as this I sometimes find it difficult to subscribe to the original argument in all its details. More especially, the references to the condition and prospects of economics and sociology in my inaugural lecture of 1938 (essay number three) no longer represent what I believe to be the present

Preface

position of the two subjects. Sociological study and writing have greatly progressed since the thirties, and my strictures of timeless and spaceless generalities of sociology no longer apply. On the other hand, the prospects of empirical and historical study and hence of practical wisdom, which I presented so hopefully in my references to the Keynesian economics, have been belied by post-war experiences. These are, however, the only points at which I find myself seriously at variance with the views I held when my essays were first published. All the other divergences are small and unimportant.

M. M. P.

Peterhouse
Cambridge

March 1970

1

REASON IN SOCIAL STUDY[1]

Truth, Sir, is a cow, which will yield such people no more milk, and so they are gone to milk the bull. DR JOHNSON

I

Academic readers in this country and in France have recently been treated to several doses of conservative anti-rationalism. There are indeed signs that in political and social philosophy as well as in ethics it is again becoming fashionable to look for antidotes to reason and to find them in history, intuition and tradition. The attitude is sufficiently recent to attract the young, and its recipe is sufficiently pungent to please the jaded. I can therefore predict it a flourishing career in the next few years, and this alone makes its argument (and for all its anti-rationalism the new fashion cannot do without an argument) worth looking into. But the argument must be treated to its own medicine and considered as an historical phenomenon. For thus considered the 'new look' of political philosophy may well turn out to be a modish variant of an ancient and recurrent outline.

Distrust of reason is indeed a perennial feature of conservative thought. The appeal to tradition, as if it were the opposite of thought, or to history, as if it were the opposite of invention, have always been the favourite themes of the conservative argument on politics and state. And not only on politics and state. Conservatism, like the rationalism it attacks, is not so much a view of social organization as a version of personal life; and in matters personal the attachment to inherited moral conventions goes hand in hand with aversion from intellectual standards. To conservatives the threat of thought is one and indivisible. It spells its dangers to the established order in all its departments – political, social, ethical, aesthetic – and therefore forces upon the philosophical conservatives a bias universally and indiscriminately anti-rationalist.

In some form and in some degree this mood is always with us. Contrary

[1] Published as 'The Revulsion from Thought' in *The Cambridge Journal*, vol. I, no. 7, April 1948. It was offered as a reply to Michael Oakeshott's article against rationalism in social and political thought, *ibid.* nos. 4 and 6.

to all vulgar notions, we are all born little conservatives. As I shall have to stress again, all social existence presupposes some stable element, and all political thought must contain a justification of some part of the established order and must express a desire to maintain it. No revolution is so revolutionary as not to appeal to some anciently established ideal; similarly, no system of individual ethics is so anarchic as not to attach itself to some conventional principle of good. But even if the conservative elements of non-conservative thought could at certain times remain unnoticed and unfelt, there would always be men willing to advertise their devotion to the established order. Thus in addition to the undercurrent of unrational or even anti-rational thought running deeply beneath all systems of ideas, there will always exist surface pools, however small and stagnant, of doctrines openly and wholly anti-rational.

The anti-rational mood is thus endemic, but at times it can assume every aspect of an epidemic. In certain historical situations the distrust of reason from being the philosophy of the few becomes the conviction of the many; and doubts about the omnipotence of reason, hitherto mere saving clauses of rational argument, begin to stalk the world as major propositions. Historians, with their gift for carving out epochs and giving them names, have called historical situations like these 'periods of romantic reaction'. Romantic is perhaps too inaccurate an adjective, but there is no doubt about the accuracy of the noun. The conservative situation is always a reaction (though to avoid the political opprobrium attaching to the word, I am going to call it 'revulsion'). It derives its inspiration and its substance from the dislike of change.

To this extent the anti-rational condition, if not wholly pathological, is at least hypochondriacal; and of the two situations the rational is the less morbid. For the rational outlook is not formed by thinking about thought; it is merely implied in the reasoned answers to individual problems. And if, in a paraphrase of Carlyle's, the end of philosophy is not thought but man's action, it is not the function of philosophy to inquire into itself – at any rate as long as all goes well with action. It is only when acts founded in reason have ended in misfortune, or have raised an inner conflict, that the ethical person begins to question his very ability to decide his conduct for himself. And it is when political decisions and political actions have brought failure, disaster and conflict, that human mind turns against its own works and stages a kind of palace revolution against itself.

Periods of great intellectual and political unsettlement, of painful or disastrous revolutions, are thus almost invariably succeeded by periods of conservative revulsion. Every schoolboy knows that one such period followed the French Revolution; and a discerning man may discover one or two such states both before and after the eighteenth century. One of them may perhaps have occurred some time in the late sixteenth and seventeenth centuries, when the counter-reformation in both its manifestations, the catholic and the calvinist, established itself over the minds of men: perhaps earlier still, when in the fourteenth century the leaders of canonist orthodoxy and Dominican conformity succeeded in laying the moral and intellectual turbulence of the thirteenth century. But even if it were too fanciful to read into the religious controversies of the middle ages and the reformation the intellectual problems of our own day, there would still be little doubt about the revulsive nature of conservatism of the nineteenth century and of our own time.

When, at the beginning of the nineteenth century, Savigny and Puchta ushered in the historical and conservative theory of law, they were not thereby propounding an independent and timeless doctrine. They were impelled by their recent recollections, by the regrettable attempts of Montesquieu's pupils to construct systems of law, and by the even more regrettable attempts of Napoleon to enact them. When at the same time Bonald and de Maistre appealed to the ancient wisdom of hereditary monarchy and the historical church, the verities they sought were not those which Aristotle had ascribed to the monarchy, and not those which Hildebrand had claimed for the Church. They were verities which offered the most potent antidote to revolution. Similarly, when less than a generation later the German economists, Knies, List, Roscher and their innumerable followers, proclaimed the birth of the historical school of political economy – a school which undertook to eschew the logical and dialectical exercises of Adam Smith and the physiocrats, and sought guidance from the economic experience of German history – they were merely reacting, and reacting violently, against the economic revolution, of which the classical and rational school of political economy approved, and against the *laisser-faire* policies, which it inspired.

The same also holds of the subsequent outbursts of anti-rationalism. Gobineau was in full flight from the bourgeois democracy of France; a couple of generations later Georges Valois and Charles Maurras led a similar flight from social democracy; Pobedonostsev, Riazanov, Bulgakov, and all the other leaders of Russian neo-orthodoxy were in spiritual resistance to the revolutionary currents of 1905. Such thoughts as the Nazis generated – and even they generated a few – also contained all the elements of a conservative revulsion. The main inspiration of Rosenberg's

3

writings was anti-Bolshevik and, to that extent, Baltic; but judged at second hand it embodied most of the reactionary German arguments against the Gotha programme and the Weimar republic. No wonder its recipe contained all the ancient ingredients of German romanticism – the appeal to intuition against reason, blood against intellect, communion with the people against personal judgment.[1]

Thus placed against the historical background of European tradition the recent manifestations of anti-rationalism fall at once into the right place in intellectual genealogy. Their faces are like many others in the family album, and even their dress comes from the family heirlooms. Now, as so many times before, the family is cashing in on the bankruptcy of the age, on the failure of the perfectionist world of the 1920s, and still more on the collapsing vision of the post-war millennium. So once again the purpose of political argument is to banish argument from politics, and once again the resources of reason are mustered to prove that reason has no resources. The mood is thus again one of revulsion, and the argument a mere antithesis. What is more, it is an antithesis to a thesis too disliked to be properly understood.

II

All this is obvious to the point of being trivial: but like all historical demonstrations it does not prove very much and disproves even less. For the case against rationalism, unlike its occasion, owes less to historical circumstance than to certain permanent themes of European culture. As I have said, distrust of thought is endemic in the history of thought, and the ideas on which it is based are part and parcel of that limited armoury of ideas with which the Almighty furnished Adam on the sixth day of creation. It is as a rule compounded of two arguments differing in range and depth. One is essentially polemical and tactical, bent on refutation, and therefore bearing more openly its aspect of revulsion; the other is more positive in that it suggests an alternative system of ideas. It is thanks to this system that the purely revulsive nature of conservative ideology so often fails to be observed.

In its short range and on its polemical side the anti-rationalist argument commonly descends to the familiar technique of the fictitious adversary. An impartial student of ideas will not fail to notice to what extent the

[1] Mr Oakeshott's rationalist is a composite monster; but ideology is one of his hallmarks; this presumably is the reason why Mr Oakeshott insists on treating the Nazis as rationalists. If so, there must be something wrong either with his definition of rationalism or with his definition of ideology, or with both.

efficacy of the anti-rationalist case depends upon intellectual misdeeds which rationalists do not in fact commit. In reading Savigny it is sometimes impossible to believe that the rationalist notions of law he so brilliantly destroyed had never existed. Lawyers are of course apt to delude themselves and others into believing that law is entirely compounded of reason. Even the English lawyers, even the founders of the common law, might give expression to some such pretensions. We all know Sir John Powell's proud dictum that 'nothing is law that is not reason'. And even Sir Edward Coke, that minor prophet of precedent and tradition, could claim not only that 'law is the perfection of reason', but also the reverse, that 'reason is the life of law'. Pretension to pure reason is indeed an occupational delusion of the legal profession. But need historians and philosophers share it? In the whole history of legal thought it is impossible to find more than a couple or so of great lawyers who in fact based their legal systems on reason and nothing but reason. There was Bentham; there was perhaps Beccaria. Some of us may have also heard about the more recent miracles of disembodied reason in the legal system of Herr Kelsen. But they were not and, apart from Beccaria, could not, on chronological grounds alone, have been the real quarry of Savigny's hounds. What they were out to catch and savage were the legal reforms and constitutional projects of the revolutionary and Napoleonic age in Germany, and they blamed them on Montesquieu, Rousseau and Condorcet. Yet what historian would ascribe to these men the pure doctrine of rational law of Savigny's imagining! After an interval of 200 years *L'Esprit des Lois* reads as an anticipation of the relativist theory of jurisprudence rather than as a plea for abstract reason in law. Read without prejudice it will inevitably suggest to the modern reader an essentially conservative view of law and society.

Similarly the *bêtes noirs* of the historical school of political economy, Say and Adam Smith, were in many ways more conservative and certainly more historical than their critics. Say, like the rest of the physiocrats, concealed behind the garb of rationalist syllogism the unquestioning attachment to the economic tradition of rural and agricultural France. In fact, his attachment to history was more intimate and less rational than that of his German 'historical' critics, so conscious of their historical evidence and so determined to rationalize it. Adam Smith was fundamentally more detached from tradition than Say. Yet, for all his Scottish background and education, his values were uncritically Anglo-Saxon and his method was as fully historical as that of any historian. Reckoned by the printer's measure, the historical argument forms a larger proportion of the *Wealth of Nations* than it does in List's *System of National Economy*.

But no image can be more fictitious than that of Rousseau as we find it in French conservative writings of the early nineteenth century. Judged by their outlook *in toto*, and not by particular arguments, Rousseau the perfectionist and Chateaubriand the reactionary (and Rousseau's adversary) were much nearer to each other than either was to any other political writer of the late eighteenth or early nineteenth century. Both were driven by the emotional turbulence within themselves into a state of revolt; both defended the free and natural man against law and politics as they found them. It so happened that Chateaubriand found the revolution all round him and therefore enlisted his wild man in the service of Church and King; while Rousseau's *milieu* was that of the *ancien régime* and his message therefore became revolutionary. Yet he was no more of a rationalist than Chateaubriand. Childe Harold knew him well: 'the self-torturing sophist, wild Rousseau.'

Indeed, it is doubtful whether the rationalists whom the anti-rationalists habitually attack have ever had an influence great enough to deserve the attention the anti-rationalists give them. Men who believe in pure reason to the extent of offering rational explanations for the universe in its entirety or who base all action on intellectual concepts will not be found at large anywhere outside a few Geneva *salons* of the eighteenth century, or the provincial debating societies of the time when H. G. Wells was young, or the RPA. Doubtless the historian, hunting among the humdrum and the second rate, may find in all places and in all ages philosophers *à la* Hudibras, who 'for every why had a wherefore'. Perhaps the Encyclopaedists were of this type; though even some of them proved their rationalism by selecting subjects, mostly those of mechanics and natural sciences, which were capable of being wholly resolved by reason; and not by forcing explanations wholly rational on every subject under the sun.

In fact, the out-and-out rationalist is a man of straw; most of the great figures in the history of thought commonly classified as rationalist are surprisingly free from the sin of exclusive intellectualism. As a group, they are what they are not by virtue of the claims they make for reason, but by virtue of the reasonable argument which they apply to problems to which reason applies. They ply a rational trade, they do not propound a rationalist metaphysic. Who was it who said (I think it was Rathenau) that by sticking to his last a cobbler does not thereby wish to demonstrate that the universe is made of leather? When it comes to actual claims on behalf of reason, to the defences of reason against faith, or to epistomo-logical argument about argument, the thought of men commonly labelled as rationalists is, as a rule, far less simple than the anti-rationalist indict-ment might suggest. Thinkers who use reason, and who rely on it, can on the whole be trusted to know how far reason can or cannot be relied upon. The record of the so-called rationalist thought is haunted by the awareness of reason's frontiers: a fact which even Lecky's history cannot wholly obscure and which even a brief historical survey will show.

III

Whether there was any philosophical rationalism in the middle ages or not, claims on behalf of the intellect, and very exalted ones at that, were made throughout the middle ages. From Gottschalk and Berengar to the Averroists it is possible to trace a continuous tradition of philosophical intellectualism asserting the right and the power of human argument. But to assert the rights of reason did not necessarily mean erecting it into an alternative to faith. To St Augustine reason was part of divine order and its exercise was a form of revelation: so to speak a revelation supple-mentary disclosing and amplifying the revelation primary. To other men less orthodox and further removed from the fountain heads of medieval orthodoxy, reason may have had a meaning nearer to our own and more sharply differentiated from faith and revelation. Yet even they did not as a rule claim for reason exclusive dominion over man's spiritual activities or over his conduct. The furthest limits of the rationalist claim in the middle ages was that of the 'double truth', i.e. the claim that philo-sophical truth was as valid within its sphere as truth vouchsafed by revelation was in religion. Even the extreme advocates of double truth, even the worldly and sceptical Averroists of Padua, did not refuse to render unto faith what was faith's and did not claim for rational argument the entire province traditionally religious. All they claimed was the right to ply their logic in fields where they thought logic could be plied.

The notion of double truth remained the established tradition of European intellectualism to our own day. Bacon may have thought he had discovered something in the nature of an intellectual technique for the manipulation of problems of natural philosophy; but what reader of Bacon will ever find him asserting that his empirical method was capable of disclosing all the mysteries of natural philosophy or that natural philosophy comprised all the mysteries of the universe? He knew that there was 'superstition in avoiding superstition'; that there was 'nothing

7

more fabulous and unbelievable than that universal frame was without mind'. And he denied that 'God and the permanence of the universe are the truth which depth of philosophy bringeth'. If these themes are not blazed forth in *Novum Organum*, this is merely because *Novum Organum* was an essay on natural phenomena. And those who having read it conclude that experimental technique was all there was to Bacon might again be reminded about the cobbler and the leathery universe.

There is no need to labour this point in relation to Descartes. The founders of the scientific philosophy of the seventeenth century, like the seventeenth-century scientists themselves, never claimed for reason universal dominion and never themselves trespassed its agreed frontiers. It is now generally accepted that Descartes and Harvey, especially the latter, were rooted in medieval scholastic tradition more deeply than behoves even a moderate rationalist; and were wont to render unto faith many a tribute that might just as well have been reserved for reason. Similarly, if Newton's outlook were viewed as a whole, no one could ever accuse him of a superstition of avoiding superstition. In the time-table of his life as in the scale of his personal values, the laws of gravitation, the theory of light and all the mathematical paraphernalia attaching to them, were no more than specialized inquiries into regions where mathematical reason had entry. Elsewhere the Bible and its fable were his guide.

What is so abundantly true of the origin of European rationalism is equally true of its age of maturity in the mid-nineteenth century. There is no denying the first half of the nineteenth century produced some important men who were fired by an intellectual optimism which may strike us now as excessive. There was Bentham, Comte and perhaps Spencer;[1] and there was of course Marx himself. The hard and glittering crust of Marx's intellectualism is there for all to behold. His lavish and self-adulatory use of the word 'scientific', the certitude and finality of his rationalism, were later to be echoed in the writings of Marxist propagandists: Engels, Bebel and a multitude of smaller fry. Indeed, no school of European thought was so aggressively rationalist; and no other school had gone so far in reducing all intellectual approaches to what Mr Oakeshott appears to mean by 'technique'.

Yet how complete and how permanent was in fact Marxist intellectualism? Marx's own attitude to concrete problems of society and

[1] Probably the out-and-out materialists, especially the Germans of Bruckner's and Mach's school, and the Russians of Pisarev's, should be classified with the rationalists. This will swell their number, but will hardly increase their weight in the history of political and social ideas. Such permanent influence as these materialists have had is almost entirely due to the love-hatred which the Marxists have conceived for them.

politics was shot through with the rose-pink hue of contemporary liberalism, largely sentimental, curiously uncritical, and fundamentally at variance with the anti-liberal bias of the Communist manifesto.[1] And before long the sentimental digressions, which, in Marx's own life and in relation to his own system, were no more than minor inconsistencies, entered into the main stream of Marxian thought and practice. In all the countries where Marxists became a political force, the very need to think out and work out its practical implications led them to import a great deal of foreign matter, some of it highly unrationalistic. In Germany the growth of socialism at the turn of the nineteenth and twentieth centuries and the political responsibilities thrust upon it after the collapse of Bismarck's repressive measures produced the back-to-Kant movement within the Marxist ranks. Its argument is familiar. Marxist dialectic was insufficient to provide the complete justification of the socialist ideal or the practical guide to socialist activity; so the absolute moral precept, the traditional notions of good and bad, truth and justice, had to be called in.

However, by far the most remarkable is the metamorphosis which has occurred in Russia in our own time. The journalists may still follow the Soviet authorities in describing the official theory and doctrine as Marxist and may still think that the formula, Marxist-Leninist-Stalinist, summarizes the logical evolution of fundamentally the same idea. Few serious students of communism will be thus taken in. No doubt the sociological terminology is still Marxist just as the official political phraseology is democratic and as the language of the constitution is liberal and individualistic. But stripped of its verbiage the Russian communism reveals itself as non-Marxist as it is anti-democratic. The Soviet conception of the Party, the store they lay by propaganda and heroic example, their emphasis on education and youth movement, to say nothing of their choice of countries to be socialized, cannot be easily fitted into a consistent system of ideas except on a view of personal behaviour, of human motivation and of historical causation much nearer to what must have been the outlook of the 'Utopian' socialists of 1840 (or of Jesuit missionaries in South American colonies of the seventeenth century) than to the world of ideas of the Marxist emigration in Geneva of 1910.[2]

[1] I have tried to show this at somewhat greater length in an essay in *The Great Democrats*, 1934, reprinted below, pp. 154–68.

[2] The rationalists in this brief survey have not been classified in accordance with Mr Oakeshott's definitions (ideology, technique, etc.). The latter are part of Mr Oakeshott's private vocabulary and cannot safely be employed by an outsider. I have used the more commonly accepted criteria. Hence the occasional differences in the two collections.

Fact and relevance

In short, the image of the rationalist as we find him in the black bestiary of the conservative anti-rationalists is a figment of their terrified imagination. For one thing, the average rationalist has been less doctrinaire than the critics make him out, and than the critics themselves often are. Whereas mystics, prophets and poets can without difficulty capture that elusive bluebird of philosophical monism and attach themselves to a single source of ideas and an all-embracing rule of conduct, students treading the hard path of intellectual inquiry are often compelled by the nature of their trade to eschew unified ideologies. The intellectual method must start and end with things outside its reach. An axiomatic postulate must be the starting point of every intellectual process; and some residium yet unresolved must also remain at the end of most inquiries reasonably conducted.

Therein lies the main intellectual difficulty of the revulsive anti-rationalists. If attack they must, they prefer to attack the out-and-out rationalist, the extremist of reason. When it comes to long-range arguments, the more intelligent rationalists might themselves be found disapproving of reason, if it happens to be taken in over-large doses. On its part conservative anti-rationalism could be as half-hearted in its denial of reason as rationalism is in its confirmation. The great conservative theoretician – a Gobineau, a Pobedonostsev, or a Pareto – is far from refusing intellect its place in the established order of the universe. Pareto for one was himself too proficient in the exercise of thought to fall into the obvious errors of solipsism. On the purely practical plane both he and the others admitted reason to society provided it was not equally distributed. It was a highly dangerous instrument and its use had to be therefore confined to the few. Gobineau and to some extent Pobedonostsev would allow the exercise of thought to the men whom they also allowed the possession of weapons; Pareto might treat it as a toxic substance and by implication allow its unrestricted use to doctors like himself, who knew the lethal dose. Podedonostsev would thus restrict its use to the autocrat, Gobineau to the ruling class, Pareto to Pareto; but none of them would deny its power or spurn its service.

The doctrine of anti-rationalism in its moderate and philosophic formulation might concede to reason a greater place still. The most important and philosophically the most respectable of the anti-rationalist arguments is that which divides the universe into spheres which belong to reason and those which do not. In its commonest version it distinguishes the world of human actions from that of physical phenomena and then proceeds to carry the distinction into the process of knowledge itself. Whereas human understanding of the physical world follows the ordinary processes of reason (or what some people prefer to call scientific method) the understanding of man and society cannot be thus attained. The physical world may be analysed into uniformities ('things have habits'); the uniformities can be expressed in laws; and laws can be employed as guides to action (Mr Oakeshott's 'technique'). But in the world of human relations, the divine cause, the free will, and the very possibility of fore-warning knowledge, defeat all attempts to discover predictable uniformities. The law of man and society is therefore of the same order as the legal law: not the generalized habits of past events, but precepts for the future, moral dictates, God's wishes. Hence the futility of all social theory, of all political and social blue prints. Men who presume to plan merely waste their time proposing things which God alone disposes.

The dualist bias of conservative thought is almost as old as that thought itself. Its occasional anticipations can be found in the middle ages and in the seventeenth and eighteenth centuries. In a curiously inverted form it constitutes the basis of Vico's philosophy.[1] But the first and still the best exposition of the duality of knowledge as it now figures in conservative thought is Kant's. In his dichotomy 'pure' reason can yield an image of the physical world approximating more or less closely to its inner reality; to the *Dinge an sich*. But in the spiritual world of man, 'practical' reason alone operates. And the knowledge it yields is not of what is but of what must; it takes the form not of general proposition framed by categories of reason but of the 'categorical imperatives' derived from the nature of man and from the will of God.

From the Kantian dichotomy have descended all the similar distinctions subsequently elaborated by later and smaller men. The more recently fabricated theories about the 'limits of scientific knowledge' (*Die Grenzen der Naturwissenschaftlichen Erkentniss*), about the specific processes of historical and religious cognition are all variations on the master's theme.[2] From the same master's theme intelligent anti-rationalists derive their most telling arguments against reason in political thought. Whether he knows it or not every conservative critic of social sciences uses

---

[1] He also divided the universe into the physical and the human, but he reserved his agnosticism for the physical world and promised full knowledge to the human.

[2] It is very puzzling why, of all the neo- and post-Kantians who wrote on this theme, Dilthey alone should have been chosen for commendation to the British public. Rickert was more precise and nearer the main stream of orthodoxy; the Marburg philosophers were more influential.

a Kantian argument as long as he is capable of using any philosophical argument at all. By the same token, it is difficult to squeeze out of Kant any argument in support of a rational study of society. As I have already said, some German socialists have tried to make Kant do the work of a socialist. Marx knew better by choosing Hegel. For all he had to do to turn Hegel into a socialist was merely to put him on his head. But Bernstein had to decapitate Kant altogether before he was able to secularize the categorical imperative, and to make it serve the needs of the socialist argument. Indeed anti-rationalists find Kant a perfect fit, and that alone explains why he cannot suit men otherwise minded.

V

Men otherwise minded must find the whole argument beside the point. After the experience of nearly two generations of inquiries students of society know that it is in fact possible to attain positive knowledge from their study; some of it of immediate practical importance. They are well aware of the difficulties of their inquiries and of the imperfections of their results. But try as they will, they cannot identify the snags which trouble them with any of the conservative objections. They may have squatted on the field which the Kantians and the crypto-Kantians have reserved for other mental activities. Well, why not? The field is carrying a good crop, satisfactory to the squatter and of great practical benefit to humanity. It is not a manna, but then it has never been the object of the squatter to be humanity's sole provider. In fact he knows that such is the nature of his field and such are humanity's needs that the things he grows will never constitute a full diet, moral or intellectual. Yet at the same time he cannot see any fundamental difference between his husbandry and the husbandry which other people carry on in other fields with the anti-rationalist's full consent.

This conviction of irrelevance, though based on homely and practical grounds, is also reflected in the underlying structure of ideas. For there too the neo-Kantian and the crypto-Kantian dichotomies are utterly unrelated to the distinctions which in fact determine the scope and validity of reason in social matters. On the plane on which Kant dwelt it may be difficult to notice how irrelevant his scheme is to the problems of social study. But once the epigones begin to draw a distinction between the allegedly uniform and generic facts of physical nature, on the one hand, and the allegedly unique, unrepeatable and individual events of social life and history on the other, the irrelevance becomes patent. For the frontier they draw separates not the different compartments of the universe but merely the different mental attitudes to the universe as a whole. What makes the material fact a fit object for scientific study is that men are prepared to treat it as an instance of a generic series. What makes a social phenomenon an historical event is that men ask about it individual or, so to speak, biographical questions. But there is no reason why the process should not be reversed: why we should not ask generic questions about historical events or should not write individual biographies of physical objects. Here Spinoza's argument still holds. The fall of a brick can be treated as a mere instance of the general study of falling bricks, in which case it is a material fact and part and parcel of a scientific inquiry. But it is equally possible to conceive a special interest in a particular brick and ask why that individual brick behaved as it did at the unique moment of its fall. And the brick will then become a subject fit for an historical biography. Newton must have been confronted with something of the same choice on the famous day when he rested under the fabulous apple tree. Had he asked himself the obvious question, why did that particular apple choose that unrepeatable instant to fall on that unique head, he might have written the history of an apple. Instead of which he asked himself why apples fall and produced the theory of gravitation. The decision was not the apple's but Newton's.

Newton's decision, though apocryphal, would have been very sensible. The reason why Kant and the neo-Kantians find it so easy to confound the difference of question with the difference of object is that in fact we have been in the habit of asking scientific questions about brick and moral and historical questions about man. We do so because we thereby reap immediate profit greater than we might have obtained by inverting the method. The interest and practical use they might obtain by writing biographies of individual inanimate objects or of animals are very small compared with the intellectual returns and practical use of treating them to scientific and generalized inquiry. *Mutatis mutandis*, the significance and relevance of an ethical inquiry or the mere interest of an individual biography of a unique person or of an historical event is often greater than can be derived from similar effort expended on the scientific ordering of human and social facts – and the mental effort would certainly be less onerous. In short, the distribution of intellectual effort has been such as to create the impression that the Kantian line divides real difference of substance. What it in fact divides is the accidental distribution of human interests and inquiries.

Viewed superficially, this line of demarcation, though it is not Kant's, implies a concession to the anti-rationalist position. The rational or scientific inquiry, the search for general causes, or to use Mr Oakeshott's phrase, the making of techniques, in the world of human affairs is more difficult and immediately less remunerative than in the so-called physical world. This is mainly due to the heterogeneity of human phenomena, to the infinite variety of their aspects and to the infinite complexity of their causes. This may make it difficult for the rational inquiry to encompass the entire field of social reality. Within that field most rationalists are sufficiently modest not to occupy at any given time more than an allotment. They admit the existence of unrationalized residua; and in common with all practising students they also admit the existence of dogmatic assumptions and intuitive judgments in all arguments and in all branches of thought, even in physics and mathematics. They may even be prepared to go as far as to say that in most human problems the elements extra- and super-rational still account for the greater part of the riddle. But they would deny that there are any departments in the universe whose riddles are so wholly beyond reason as to be utterly inaccessible to rational thought. The very idea of God and religious experience are not barred to rational inquiry. Even if the reality of God were accepted dogmatically and the whole creed taken as revealed, there would still remain within religious experience a vast field for reason and room even for the much-despised 'techniques'. Indeed, what is theology if not a product of rational thought operating in those branches of religious knowledge in which rational thought can usefully operate.

Therein lies the rationalist answer to the conservative doubt. He cannot be accused of trying to solve by syllogism or by laboratory experiment every problem of the universe and to base on them every rule of conduct. The history of rational thought, as distinct from the history of rationalist claims, is a record of study which reason proved capable of undertaking, not a history of attempts to pack the entire universe into a technical formula. The rationalist admits that there are questions to which he cannot give a complete and final answer, but he also claims that there are few questions to the understanding of which he cannot make some contribution, however small.

2

HISTORY AND THE SOCIAL SCIENCES[1]

I

The place of history in the social sciences appears much more doubtful to the historians than to the social scientists. The latter recognize, and indeed strive for, generalizations impartially derived from history as well as from anthropology and statistical sociology. They may still disagree as to whether the theoretical manipulation of social data should be in the hands of those who collect them, i.e. the historian, the anthropologist and the statistician, or whether a special body of sociologists is necessary to co-ordinate and generalize from facts which other social sciences gather. But there is no disagreement about the need and the possibility of employing social evidence, including historical evidence, for theoretical purposes.

Some fifty to seventy-five years ago this point of view would not have appeared as exceptionally controversial even to the historian. In the heroic age of historical writing, when the main outlines of European historiography were for the first time drawn, history was studied chiefly for the sake of the lessons it taught, or, in other words, for the sake of the generalizations it suggested. It was only in the nineteenth century that a reaction developed against universal historical laws. In the beginning the reaction was a half-hearted one. Men like de Maistre or Savigny were even more anxious to learn from history than Voltaire or Montesquieu had been. Where they differed from the eighteenth-century rationalists was in their insistence on the peculiarity of historical generalizations, their local and temporal relativity. But as the century drew on it became more and more fashionable for historians to profess a dislike of generalizations, even of specifically historical ones. Some of the dislike had its source in the philosophical reaction to the progress of science. Aided by the Kantian distinction between pure and practical reason, philosophers succeeded in spreading the view of history as an impregnable stronghold of non-

[1] A paper read to the conference on Social Sciences held in 1935 at Bedford College, London, and first published in *The Social Sciences: Their Relations in Theory and Teaching* (London, 1936).

scientific knowledge. But Neo-Kantian philosophy was not the only and not even the most important source of the anti-scientific reaction in modern historiography. Much more important has been the organic development of historical study itself. The very success of the early masters in drawing a full outline of European development has forced upon their successors the task of mere correction and verification, and has turned the whole attention of working historians to the minor blemishes in the old generalizations. This critical attitude to minutiae has become in the end a powerful agent of selection. It now attracts to history persons of a cautious and painstaking disposition, not necessarily endowed with any aptitude for theoretical synthesis. No wonder the flight from generalization has been gathering speed. Ranke's famous formula, 'wie es wirklich war', was not, at the time of its conception, meant to be anything more than an appeal for the suspension of generalizations until more was known about facts. But by degrees it has come to symbolize the repudiation of all theoretical interests. If historians nowadays achieve anything different from mere description, they usually do so in spite of their avowed intention 'to confine themselves to facts'. Whatever the actual performance, the official programme of modern history is the search for facts for their own sake.

There still remain historians for whom the satisfactions of archivist research are not sufficient to justify the existence of their study. Some of them try to give their subject a higher meaning by placing it beyond science: to them history is an emotional and artistic exercise, aiming at the intuitive comprehension of concrete situations or whole epochs. But on the whole even they have failed to impose their aims on the main body of working historians. To a historian 'artistic' history means well-written history, just as 'scientific' history means accurate history – a misuse of terms which merely illustrate the intellectual state of modern historiography.

II

If history is to regain its place in the general intellectual movement of our time, it must restore to the full its erstwhile connection with social generalizations. Some such connection is always present. Social facts, like all other facts, are not concrete and complete phenomena with a real and objective existence, but merely 'relevances', aspects of reality relating to the interests of the observer. Descriptive historians, like all observers of reality, are, often without knowing it, merely engaged in the selection of 'relevant aspects'. Where they differ from the social scientists is in that the aspects they select are relevant not to the problems of social science, but to something else. As often as not that 'something else' is provided by the theoretical interests of the nineteenth-century historians. Modern constitutional historians preoccupied with the minutiae of royal pre-rogative, representative government and legislative procedure, still continue to serve those political problems which engaged the attention of statesmen and political philosophers at the time when the foundations of modern constitutional history were being laid. Modern economic historians engrossed in the manor, the personal status of peasants, the guilds, the mercantilist policy, owe their subjects to the early-nineteenth-century preoccupation with the problems of legal and commercial freedom. Even in those branches of political history which are most concerned with concrete and picturesque phenomena, the biographies and the military campaigns, the selection of topics is still determined by the political and theoretical inquiries of past centuries. By refusing to teach new lessons history merely succeeds in repeating old ones.

III

It is very largely in order to rid history of scientific implications, new or old, that the ideal of history as art or as a branch of ethics has been put before historians. By itself the ideal need not exclude the claims of scientific history, any more than the insistence on sociological generaliza-tion excludes the claims of history as an art. But in recent discussion, especially among Neo-Kantian philosophers, to insist on history as an art has become merely a way of saying that it cannot be a science. In trying to reveal the mission of history as a vehicle of specific forms of cognition, the philosophers are merely trying to prove that it cannot be an object of ordinary rational and positive knowledge.

The arguments which are usually invoked for the purpose are perhaps too familiar to be reproduced and criticized here at length, especially as most of them reach beyond history to the whole problem of social sciences. If they are mentioned here at all it is only because they are supposed to apply with special force to history, and because some of them do indeed touch upon the real peculiarities of the historical method.

Two groups of argument are most commonly employed, one which is largely invalid and one which embodies what is now a generally admitted criticism. The invalid argument emphasizes the 'unique and unrepeatable' character of historical occurrences and the consequent opposition between the historical description of events and the scientific search for general laws. In its simplest form this argument confuses the things historians actually do with the things history can or should do. As will be shown further, the preoccupation of historians with unique events is very largely fictitious, but, even if it were genuine, the fact that historians are thus occupied would by itself prove nothing about the nature of history. The fact that historians are dealing with unique events does not mean that history cannot be studied for any other purpose or in any other way. It can of course be argued that historians are forced to engage in the study of unique occurrences by the nature of historical reality. But, however relevant, this argument would be inconclusive, and from the idealist point of view also inconsistent. It is now well understood that social experience is not the only repository of unique events, and there is no need now to repeat Spinoza's famous demonstration of the unique and unrepeatable nature of events in physical reality. If physical scientists have succeeded in discovering the uniformity of nature, they have done so because from the very beginning they turned away from the unique and the unrepeatable to the common and the generic. In the same way the possibility of social science, and of scientific generalization in history, turns on whether the historian like the physicist is willing to subordinate his study of the unique to his search for the general.

Much more serious and more valid is the criticism which deals with the subtlety and complexity of social experience. The difficulties here stressed are practical rather than epistemological. The sociologist's instruments of abstraction, above all his language, are so crude, and his relation to social facts is so intimate, that he may never succeed in emulating the physicist and resolving social life into simple generalized aspects. Even if he does, social life is too complex, and the number of facts is too enormous, for him to be able to solve social equations in their entirety, and thus to achieve control over concrete social phenomena.

There is no denying the relevance of this criticism. Yet however real it is, its destructive effects should not be exaggerated. In the first place what it attacks is not the possibility of social science but the possibility of social technology. Its real target is the naive mid-Victorian 'lesson of history'. That 'lesson' was not theoretical but applied, and was meant to apply to complete social events instead of their generalized aspects. But what is an argument against premature and naive attempts at social engineering, is not necessarily an argument against attempts at a social science. Control over reality may be the driving impulse and perhaps even the true end of science, but the perfection of the control is not and cannot be a preliminary test of scientific status.

In the second place this criticism does not altogether destroy the value of historical generalization, however indefinite and incomplete, even to the social engineer. Social science may be capable only of imperfect answers, but even imperfect answers have technological value. Perfect prediction is impossible until all the factors in the social equation have been resolved, but perfect prediction is not the only alternative to no prediction at all. Every addition to our generalized knowledge of society, however vague and however small, is a contribution to our powers of social control. Every social generalization successfully constructed is a step away from the infinite expectations of an infant, or of a culture at its pre-scientific stage, and a step towards the more limited range of expectation of a man 'wise' about life, or of a generation in the possession of an ordered and classified social experience.

IV

The real significance of this group of objections, however, lies in its bearing upon the procedure and method of scientific history. On the way to social generalizations, mere approximations are not to be spurned, yet no mere approximation can be given the verbal form of law. No laws except perfect ones bear being put into words. It is the premature use of universal terms that has earned for general sociology much of its past ill repute. To this incapacity for scientific articulation history must, and in fact does, reconcile itself. Its scientific questions and its generalized answers are and should be implied rather than stated. The procedure is not without its dangers. With its theoretical preoccupations veiled, scientific history may sometimes be confused with the descriptive work of the archivist and the story-teller. But fictitious similarities of this kind are inevitable, and as long as they are fictitious they are essential to scientific history and to the place it occupies in social science.

One of the fictitious similarities is that of 'concreteness'. Even if and when the real interest of the student and his conscious preoccupation is with a general inquiry, he gives his subject not the form of a general question and a general answer, but that of a concrete study of a single event. Though Weber's real preoccupation was with the general correlation of religious ideas and economic development, the ostensible subject of his investigation was the concrete phenomenon of puritan ideas in the economic evolution of the seventeenth and eighteenth centuries. McIlwain's well-known work is a study of the transformation of custom into law, but his avowed subject is a certain phase in the legal and constitutional development in the middle ages. The garb of fictitious concreteness may sometimes be so thick that the underlying implications may remain invisible to the author himself, and many a respectable historian would be shocked to find that he wrote sociology. Yet it is almost invariably the fictitious nature of the 'concreteness' that makes a historical work 'interesting' to the student. Wherever the 'concreteness' of the phenomena described is not fictitious but real, the account almost invariably loses its appeal to the intellect. To use a common expression it ceases to be 'suggestive'; to use a more exact one, it ceases to be science.

Another fictitious similarity is that of 'uniqueness'. It is impossible to derive a sociological generalization from a single concrete event. A generalization to be valid must be based on the familiar procedure of the comparative method. Such, however, is the complexity of historical data and so subtle are the differences and the similarities, that most of the efforts of historians and sociologists to engage in explicit comparisons have turned out to be crude and naive. Where they have succeeded, it is only with the assistance of a fictitious 'uniqueness' – a pretence that one situation at one point of time and one point of space is being studied. As in the case of writing which is fictitiously 'concrete', the fictitious character of historical uniqueness may also remain unnoticed by the writers themselves. Tacitus may have believed that what he was describing were the manners of the Germans and not of his fellow Romans. In reality the bulk of modern work on medieval economic history, most recent European work on the history of Greek religion, a great deal of French and German work on ancient social and constitutional history, is shot through with comparison. Wherever historical investigation makes an appeal to intelligence, there is almost always an implied comparison with some other epoch, mostly our own, and an implied comparison with other places, mostly foreign.

It is this 'fictitious' procedure of scientific history that the Neo-Kantian critics have failed to understand, and this failure largely explains the manner in which they discuss not only what history can do, but what history does. The procedure must also be understood by historians, if they are not to be impaled on the horns of the dilemma which the philosophical critics have revealed. It is very easy for a historian to become either a 'general sociologist' or an antiquarian. Scientific history is neither, and the way to it lies through this fictitious procedure as reflected in the choice and formulation of historical subjects. Unlike the macrocosmic subjects of the general sociologist and the microscopic subjects of the antiquarian, those of the historian are microcosmic. General sociology, with its taste for vast campaigns and its indifference to minor obstacles, sometimes tries to arrive at its generalizations by a frontal attack. When such sociologist wants to investigate the relation between religion and ethics, he may write about religion and ethics through all time and space. At the other extreme is the antiquarian, who placates his intellectual agoraphobia by shutting himself up in small and dark subjects. The microcosmic method of a scientific historian implies a recognition of the need for making his investigations relevant to the wider issues of social science and a yet further recognition of the special difficulties and peculiar shortcomings of social investigation.

3

THE HISTORICAL METHOD IN SOCIAL SCIENCE[1]

Few other branches of university study are more indigenous to Cambridge than the one which I have the great honour to represent. It was in Cambridge that Archdeacon Cunningham laid the foundations of economic history as a university subject, and it was out of this University that the long stream of his pioneer books issued. Cunningham was a great missionary, for economic history was to him part of his political and philosophical faith. He believed that English thought, and English politics of his time, wanted rescuing from the a-moral and a-national prejudices of liberal economics and whig history; and it was from economic history as then taught in Germany that the cure would come. This belief led him to concentrate very largely on the problems of economic policy to the exclusion of many of the topics which form the scope of economic history now. Yet it is remarkable how, in spite of his preoccupations, the work has survived the faith which prompted it and in its main outlines endures to our own day. If economic historians of the next generation were able to devote themselves to specialized study, it was because the field was occupied for them and the foundation laid by Cunningham.

But what the generation which followed owed to the man who laid the foundation, the present generation owes to the man who built on them: the first holder of the Chair, the master mason who has preceded me. On the ground on which Dr Clapham has worked and still works he found a mass of half-knowledge, overgrown with picturesque and stubborn weeds. This ground he has not only cleared, but in his own inimitable, lapidary way, has covered with a structure of facts as hard and certain as granite. On his ground and in his manner nothing else remains to be done: so in Cambridge where the first phase of economic history was begun, the second has just been concluded.

[1] An inaugural lecture, Cambridge, 1938, published by the Cambridge University Press in 1939.

The historical method in social science

With these achievements to precede him, no present holder of the Chair can claim to be a pioneer. He will never know the joy of staking out the first claims and of turning the first sod, or the greatest of all joys, that of inventing new names. Yet he will be a hypocrite if he pretends not to relish the advantages of his position as an inheritor; above all, the great advantage of being able not to engage in his inaugural lecture in the great controversy of history as science *versus* history as art.

In so far as science means accuracy, and art good writing, their respective claims on historians have now been settled, for we all now agree with the Regius Professor that history should be both accurate and readable. But even if both science and art are defined by their objects – science as a search for general causes, art as an exercise in imaginative creation – the issue does not present itself to economic history, though it may still concern other branches of history. For in economic history the practices of its founders, the accident of its rise and the nature of its material, deprive the historian of real choice and condemn him to dwell with the social sciences.

The facts of economic history cannot be shaped, as a personal biography or a field of battle can, into an image with a direct appeal to our artistic sensibilities. Its most effective instrument, as Dr Clapham has so well argued and proved, is the impersonal language of statistical measurements. It came into existence not as an attempt to rival the novel or the drama in the recreation of life, but as an endeavour to assist in the solution of social problems. Its founders abroad were lawyer-sociologists of the romantic period, Möser, Guizot, Lamprecht, or the economists of the mid-century, Knies, Roscher, List. Its source of inspiration in this country is Adam Smith, and its ethos derives more from Bacon than from Shakespeare. So, much as economic historians would like to rank with the richest and oldest of the arts, they are compelled to serve the poorest and the youngest of sciences.

But for one controversy they have escaped they have raised legions of others. Having gone to dwell with the social sciences they have still to decide the details of the dwelling: what it is to be – detached or semi-detached, and where – in the public halls or the servants' quarters. All these are problems of cohabitation within the social sciences, and the very fact that the sites have not yet been completely marked out makes the choice uncertain and difficult.

Regarded superficially, the mood now prevailing among history's nearest neighbours is very propitious to economic and social history. A new wave of empiricism appears to be sweeping across regions hitherto inhabited by pure theory. The most general, and the least defined of social studies, sociology, is rapidly winding up its interest in comprehensive formulae and is turning into a comparative study of institutions: family, property, legal custom, class division. When done expertly, it merges into the specialized study of social evidence; and since all social evidence, where it is not anthropological or statistical, is bound to be historical, much of sociology has been assuming the character of generalized and universalized history. Similarly, what now passes for political science is in large part concerned with political institutions as they are revealed in recent historical experience. And finally, economics – the field in which economic historians most frequently camp – has entered into one of its empirical phases.

The economists, like the theoretical sociologists of old, only more so, tried to solve the largest possible problems from the least possible know-ledge. The ingenuity which went, and still goes, into some of the syllo-gistic exercises of theoretical economics is only rivalled by the unreality of some of its conclusions. But if some of its conclusions are capable of illuminating real problems of economic life, and economics as a whole is something more than a soufflé of whipped postulates, it is because even the most theoretical of economists sometimes manage to mix their theorems with a little social observation. The fact that the Cambridge economists, from Marshall to Keynes, have always tried to draw upon their personal observations of reality may account for the practical importance of their theoretical constructions. Marshall's capacity for interpolating a new empirical condition at each successive stage of his argument, and of calling in new facts to redress old conclusions, is perhaps the most striking feature of his method. And no reader of Keynes's general theory will fail to observe the central position occupied in it by two acutely observed empirical scales.

But what in books of Marshall or Keynes is an occasional spark of private wisdom now promises, or shall I say threatens, to become an organized branch of economic study. The realization that their subject has been purer than it ought to be has led the economists to insist upon the need for inductive study. In this country very recently, in the United States and Germany for quite a long time, an ever-growing amount of academic effort has been turned to the collection of economic facts. Studies of individual industries, of individual firms, of price and wage movements, commercial treaties and legislative methods, have been flooding the market. Measured by bulk, most American economic study is devoted to collection of facts. Similarly measured, the syllabus of the Economics Tripos in Cambridge consists very largely of courses on this or that industry, this or that region. And to listen to fashionable economic talk, one might think that the whole race of economists has become converted to the religion of the counting machine.

II

So, superficially, it would appear that history, as the repository of the empirical facts which the economist and sociologist can employ, has come to its own again, and that the social sciences are once again becoming historical. And yet, if truth be known, much of the recent hankering for facts and wooing of facts and amassing of facts, appears to an economic historian as far removed from history and as irrelevant to the real business of empirical study as are the arm-chair fantasies of the sociologists or the pure abstractions of the mathematical economists. For though in a sense all facts are historical facts, and all historical facts are social evidence, the data which the economists and sociologists now accumulate are seldom employed in a way which an economic historian would recognize as historical.

History is something which is both more and less than what sociologists and economists now make of it. It is certainly something more than an assemblage of data. We all know that what now distinguishes the honourable occupation of antiquaries from the questionable occupation of historians is that whereas antiquaries collect facts historians study problems. To a true antiquary all past facts are welcome, to an historian facts are of little value unless they are causes, or parts of causes, or the causes of causes, of the phenomena which he studies. A description of an industry wherein all the facts which strike the student's eye are assembled is a piece of economic antiquarianism. Economic history ends at the point at which the facts cease to answer questions, and the nearer the questions are to social problems and the more completely the problems dominate the search for facts, the nearer is the study to the true function of history in social science.

These obvious remarks may strike economists as an admonition delivered at a wrong address, for in the past the economists were apt to justify their indifference to historical study by the alleged irrelevance of economic history to the problems of economics. With this accusation we shall presently deal: for the alleged irrelevance of the topics of economic history is not altogether the historian's fault. But even if it were, the fact remains that the amount of useful knowledge or just ordinary sense that can be derived from the flood of empirical studies is incommensurate with the effort expended on them. And if that is so, it is not because the searchers are incompetent, the evidence intractable, or other sciences unco-operative, but because the main direction of the so-called empirical economics is at fault. The economists so seldom derive from their facts the theoretical knowledge they require because they do not ask from their facts the kind of question facts can answer.

We have just said that the nearer the question is to a social problem, the more completely it dominates a fact, so much the nearer it is to history and to the true business of social science. This economists understand only too well; what they perhaps do not realize is that for the purposes of empirical study the question, the dominating problem, is not necessarily given by the theoretical conclusions of abstract economics. The prevailing tendency among economists is to believe that, having arrived at a conclusion by a long and complicated series of deductions from original propositions, they can then proceed to verify it on historical and statistical facts. I do not want to suggest that that verification is always impossible, or where possible undesirable. In fields in which the original assumptions correspond closely to an experience which is real, easily discoverable, and limited in range, conclusions are sometimes arrived at, which subsequent empirical study can check. No reader of Taussig's book on the History of American Tariffs, or Viner's on Canada's Foreign Trade, or Bresciani-Turroni's on German Inflation, can fail to notice how well some propositions of economics can be supported by historical facts. Far be it from me to deny the possibility or the value of attempts at verification such as these. But the bulk of the empirical studies do not verify any of the conclusions of economic theory, for the simple reason that most of the conclusions are so derived as to be incapable of empirical verification, and some of them are so constructed as not to require it and to be illuminating and important even though unverifiable.

Economists have lately been only too anxious to abandon the logical position which they have so proudly occupied since the days of Ricardo, Mill, Menger, and the older Keynes. The methodological assumption and justification of theoretical economics is the belief that it covers a field of problems in which knowledge could best be acquired by the exercise of deductive reasoning. In the modest opinion of an outsider like myself, this assumption has been borne out by the history of economic science. In the fields which economists have chosen as their own, they have reaped a crop of conclusions far greater in bulk and finer in substance than anything they could have obtained by the inductive study of facts. But the price of deduction is abstraction: the logical rigour and consistency of economic propositions is a direct consequence of the fact that the fundamental concepts, the original assumptions and the successive stages of economic argument are all treated in isolation from the rest of social environment. And abstraction accounts for the unhelpfulness of economics as well as for its success. Having been derived by way of continuous and accumulated abstraction, and composed of *a priori* concepts, economic propositions cannot be directly applied to facts for purposes of either policy or verification. Within their limits they are as true as, if not truer than, any other branch of scientific knowledge. Where they are unsatisfactory is not in their being wrong but in their being incomplete. And where the empirical studies can help, is not in making them truer but in making them fuller; not so much in testing their often untestable truth on facts, as in making them more relevant and tangible by supplementing them with scientific thought on those aspects of social life from which they have been abstracted.

This residuum of social life fills the background of economic theories as a kind of invisible presence: mentioned frequently and always reverentially, but seldom studied, never analysed. Sometimes it makes a fleeting entry into an economic theorem in the famous disguise of 'other conditions being equal', only to pass out of discussion with its incognito intact. Even though the one thing we know for certain about the 'other conditions' is that they cannot possibly be equal, little is done to establish their true identity, to go behind their variety and flux, and to understand the intricacies of their pattern.

Sometimes these other conditions enter economic theory in the form of specific assumptions. Certain modes of social behaviour which are known intimately to affect the economic problem under discussion, but have not been selected for manipulation by economists, are then named, and left named, as special assumptions. So special are they that the whole practical value, the whole significance of the theorem when applied, indeed its very chance of being applied, depends on the knowledge of the modes of behaviour thus assumed. And yet the knowledge is not there, and little attempt is made to obtain it.

Thus in a recent restatement of the theory of international trade,[1] that trade is shown to be primarily 'caused by the uneven distribution of the

[1] B. Ohlin, *International Trade* (Harvard, 1935), *passim*, and especially pp. 48 and 58 and ch. XVII.

factors' of production, and important conclusions are made to depend on the interregional movements of capital and labour. But what that 'uneven distribution' was and is – its causes and prospects – is unknown and taken for granted. Similarly assumed and almost equally unknown are the all-important movements of the 'factors'. For in spite of the interesting illustrations which the author draws from his Scandinavian and American experience, and a statistical sketch of the relations between prices and foreign lending, the social processes behind the migration of capital and labour still remain unexplored and unexplained.

In the same way a generally accepted formulation of the theory of wages contains a set of propositions dependent on a number of assumed social conditions, and among them population, the supply of capital, the people's ability or willingness to work, and technical inventions.[1] The theory establishes clearly that its conclusions as to wages and employment will in each concrete case be dependent on what those social conditions happen to be. But do we know enough about the conditions to be able to give reality to the author's proposition? What social causes, psychological, political, institutional, determined in the past and are likely to go on determining the changing attitudes of labour or the changing supplies of capital or the development of applied science or the outbursts of technical ingenuity?

Or let us take an example more up-to-date and nearer Cambridge. Mr Keynes's famous general theory of employment, if I understand it correctly, makes a set of conclusions about employment, the rate of interest, and in certain contingencies also prices and wages, dependent on two scales of human behaviour: the propensities of men to consume different proportions of their income, and their preferences for the different degrees of liquidity in which savings can be held. The existence of these scales is acutely observed, their importance as concepts has been universally acknowledged, their names now belong to the basic English of economics. But how much do the economists know about them? Do they know or have they explained the complex social process which throughout history has determined the employment of income and its allocation to consumption or rather to consuming classes, or have they tried to discover what social forces lurk behind liquidity preferences?

I could multiply the examples *ad infinitum*, but I hope my meaning is clear without them. Such assumptions about the social background as are made by economists, indeed the very fact that they are made, show that they are regarded as important. The fact that although they are as yet

[1] J. R. Hicks, *A Theory of Wages* (London, 1932), p. 114.

unknown they do not block the activity of the economists shows that they are regarded as capable of being known. Why then is there so little empirical economics dealing not only with the statistical verification of economic propositions, but also with the disclosure and analysis of their social conditions?

I know that by asking this question I am inviting the retort and the advice not to be in a hurry. For what the economists have not yet done they may do yet. But if that is the retort, I should like to be allowed the dismal prophecy that the same causes which prevented the economists from engaging in these problems yesterday will prevent them both today and tomorrow. The social topics which they themselves assume, but do not settle, belong to regions of inquiry which are outside, i.e. either beyond or beneath, the typical economist's tastes and powers. They are particles of concrete and tangible reality, their study demands constant reference to the whole combination of social forces, their logical problem is that of multiple interrelation, indeed an interrelation so multiple as to make the work of abstraction impossible and undesirable. My impertinent suggestion therefore is that those fields which the economists are obviously unable or unwilling to cultivate belong to other people. They are the true regions of empirical study; and had better be left to students who specialize in complex social situations, who search for past causes (and all causes are past causes), and who above all do not expect their result ever to reach the precision of a mathematical formula, and will therefore not be disappointed by the more indeterminate results which can be derived from the study of historical reality. In short, the regions are those of economic history, and by occupying them and working them historians can make the one contribution to economic science which at present nobody else seems to be making.

III

I hope that by thus defining the character of the contribution which empirical study in general, and economic history in particular, can make to economic science, I have not given the impression of extravagance. For what I have just said about the indeterminate results of historical study recalls the statement with which I started: namely, that history is not only more but also less than the use to which it is sometimes turned by social scientists. If economists err on the side of disparagement, by limiting too narrowly the range of historical inquiry, sociologists err on the side of extravagance by exalting unduly the function of historical facts. They expect from them final and instantaneous solutions of all the most profound of society's problems. And they are convinced that if history has so far failed to yield a complete science of society and to found the engineering technique of politics, the fault is not history's but the historian's. There is an assumption throughout the whole of their recent work that in the hands of sociologists historical evidence can easily be made to yield the secrets which it refuses to historians. Hence the embarrassingly ambitious – and to an historian the embarrassingly crude – treatises on society in general, property in general, class in general, which are produced by sociologists on the basis of evidence, originally collected by historians. Hence, also, the attempts to wring from historical facts theoretical lessons, lessons which send shivers up the historian's spine for the violence they do to facts, the simplicities they impose upon life.

This aversion of historians to the maltreatment of their facts by sociologists is a result neither of stupidity nor of ignorance, but of experience and disillusionment. The historical method in social science has its own history, and that history is filled with the tombstones of historical schools, which claimed for their method more than it could give. The scientific employment of social, legal and constitutional history began in the attempts of people in the eighteenth and the early nineteenth centuries to derive from history useful political and philosophical lessons. Even the notions of historical relativity and anti-philosophical scepticism which mark the rise of the so-called historical schools of jurisprudence and politics in the early nineteenth century were tinged with the belief that where reason failed historical study might succeed. History, it was thought, could, when suitably employed, not only show up the imperfection of rational propositions but also support general propositions of its own. But the subsequent two or three generations, above all the mid-decades of the Victorian age, taught history yet another lesson. For while the historical school of jurisprudence, Savigny and the rest, found it only too easy to demonstrate the imperfection of the universal principles of rationalist jurisprudence and political theory, they have not been able to replace them with a single historical principle capable of direct general formulation. And similarly while Knies, Roscher and Schmoller found no difficulty in showing the relativity of Adam Smith's and Ricardo's ideas, and their dependence upon circumstances which were purely English and purely temporary, they were unable to derive from history anything in the nature of alternative principles capable of replacing the ones they had rejected.

So now at last the practitioners of the historical method have discovered, what its founders may not have realized, that even though historians and theoreticians travel on the same road, they not only use different vehicles, but also reach different destinations. For the destination of the theoretical sociologists – general universal laws, directly derived from empirical evidence and explicitly stated in generic terms – are things beyond the reach of the most flighty and peregrinatory of historians.

Why this is so all historians and many non-historians now realize. As I have already said, the degree of generalization which the theoretical economists have achieved in their field, and which some philosophers of law would like jurisprudence to achieve in theirs, has been made possible only at the price of abstraction. Now, history also can and also does abstract to some extent; but the extent makes all the difference. Abstraction of a sort is an essential condition of all processes of thought; without it we can use no language; the historian abstracts his facts and groups them into classes and types merely by using words. By calling the war of 1815 a 'war', and the war of 1914 a 'war', and the Punic War a 'war', the historian creates generic terms and abstracts up to a certain degree. But the degree, the length to which he is prepared to go on abstracting, is of vital importance. Beyond a certain point abstraction robs the fact of all historical reality. What gives facts of history, or all social facts, their worth as evidence, and their value for causal analysis, is their existence, their tangible and verifiable reality. Only tangible and concrete phenomena can be fitted into a social setting and demonstrated as a link in a chain of causation. But when abstraction has gone so far as entirely to separate the fact from its social environment, when the concept of war is so employed as to exclude all the historical circumstances of the war of 1815 and of that of 1914 and of the Punic War, the facts of history cease to be facts, lose their value as evidence, and the justification of history as a search for concrete causes goes.

The topics of history, however general in some of their aspects, have an individual existence, and it is for that reason that the historian, however generalizing he is by temperament and however sociological in interests, always writes biographies, accounts of single combinations of circumstances. The historian's work is biographical, even when the subject of the biography is such an impersonal and sociological phenomenon as my own subject of study at the moment: rural society in the middle ages. Where the historian shows his scientific preoccupations, and qualifies for membership of the social sciences, is in concentrating the study of his individual subject on its relevance to general and theoretical problems. He studies rural society in the middle ages, which is a unique and unrepeatable phenomenon, because the study is relevant to such sociological problems as the correlation of population, social structure, social class and tenure, economic technique and legal concepts. But unlike a sociologist he refuses to ask universal questions or try to formulate general laws.

Confronted with the same problems a sociologist would write a book on the connection between social structure and economic technique in all places and all centuries, as exhibited by historical evidence of every country and every age; he would write a similar book on all family, all class, all property. But to an historian these frontal attacks on theoretical problems, even when delivered with massed battalions of historical facts, are not history; and in my opinion they are not even social science. Social study in its empirical ranges deals with entire social patterns; however abstracted and however simplified, its facts are still too complex for a single and a simple prediction. And at the cost of yet another repetition, we must insist that the penalty of being sufficiently concrete to be real is the impossibility of being sufficiently abstract to be exact. And laws which are not exact, predictions which are not certain, generalizations which are not general, are truer when shown in a concrete instance or in one of their unique manifestations than they are when expressed in quasi-universal terms.

The only thing therefore which economic and social history can do for social science is to go on studying individual situations, rural society in thirteenth-century England, the rise of modern industry in the eighteenth-century midlands, labour's attitudes to wages and hours in the first half of the nineteenth century, technical education in Germany in the second half of the nineteenth century, the English wool-trade in the middle ages, etc., etc. But while studying social situations it must ask questions and look for answers capable of revealing the action of social causes. In studying rural society in the thirteenth century one may demonstrate the economic transformation produced by the growth of population, and in studying the labour attitude to wages one may lay bare the social forces which once converted a portion of humanity into a capitalist factor of production and still go on affecting its mobility and economic tractability. In studying technical education in Germany and the relation of factories to universities one may reveal the causes which are capable of stimulating an independent movement of technical progress. These microscopic problems of historical research can and should be made microcosmic – capable of reflecting worlds larger than themselves. It is in this reflected flicker of truth, the revelations of the general in the particular, that the contribution of the historical method to social science will be found.

Is a light so meagre worth shedding? Is it worth giving implied answers, incapable of being put into words, to assumed questions which do not suffer being asked? Is not the whole enterprise of social and economic history as part of social science a mere attempt to overcome the difficulty of scientific thought by shirking it?

These doubts are not for me to answer. Had my subject today been 'The Value of Historical Study' I should have taken refuge in the common truth that historical knowledge has a virtue which, like that of all knowledge, is independent of its value as science. But as my subject is not the virtue of history but its scientific use, I can only plead in defence the common limitations and common hopes of all social sciences. The value of the historical contribution to the science of humanity is essentially the same as that of all the other contributions: small and uncertain. Whether it is hopeful, as well as being small and in spite of being uncertain, depends on the prospect of the social sciences as a whole, and not on that of history alone. For the uncertainty of historical results is due not to their being produced by historians, but to their being based on social facts. The real question is therefore not whether it is worth the social scientist's while to take the economic historian in as a partner, but whether it is worth his while to set up in business at all. And if I personally am hopeful about the contribution of history, it is because I am not hopeless about the task of social science.

The reason why I am not hopeless is perhaps due to the fact that I am not over-ambitious. I do not believe that the science of society will ever achieve the perfection of astronomy, but neither do I think that scientific thought is impossible or useless on lower ranges of perfection. The perfect achievement of scientific endeavour is to produce in man that certainty of expectation on which action can be based. This absolute certainty is the very opposite of the infinity of possibilities which every situation presents to a savage or a child. Between the perfect astronomical anticipation of the eclipse and the ignorance of a child as to what will follow a rapid movement of hand, a temporary disappearance of the mother, there are infinite variations and degrees in the certainty of anticipation. The path of science is that of progressive reduction in the choice of expectation, and the further the choice is reduced the nearer is thought to the ideal of science and the further it is from primitive ignorance.

Few branches of science, even astronomy, can claim to have reduced all the alternative expectations to one; on the other hand I cannot imagine social studies in combination as incapable of achieving any reduction at all. No matter how much we study wars we shall perhaps never be able to formulate a single generic law as to the cause of war; similarly, no matter how much we study rural society we shall never be able to express the interdependence of population and agricultural technique in a mathematical formula. But, as long as each concrete instance is studied with relevance to real problems, the accumulated results – that is to say, the accumulated analysis of the causes at work – does, and will still more in the future, create a knowledge of society which stands in the same relation to the savage ignorance now prevailing as life's experience or life's wisdom, with its limited range of expectations, stands to the unlimited range of an infant. That position of collective wisdom or historical experience will not be a complete and a perfect science, but for that matter so few of the sciences are. We are hopeful because we are modest; we are modest because we are historians: because the experience of a century of historiography has made us wiser than we should have been a hundred years ago as to what history can and cannot do. Our science, like charity, begins at home.

4

FUNCTION AND DIALECTIC IN ECONOMIC HISTORY

The topic of this essay, frequently discussed by initiates in private, has not so far been introduced to the main body of economic historians. My decision to assume the task of introducing it has been prompted by a personal encounter with the problem. Some time ago I showed to Dr N, a younger colleague in my field, something I had written about sales of land in the villages of the twelfth and thirteenth centuries. My argument was that the village land market and the social differences it caused were to be found in all the periods of the Middle Ages for which there is evidence.[2] The conclusion aroused my colleague to a rueful comment that if I were right – and he appeared to think that I was – the outcome of my study, like that of other such studies, might be to create the impression that English society never changed; and where there was no change there was no history.

This is, of course, a real problem. Its reality may not seem apparent to the straight historians, i.e. those who mainly occupy themselves with political narrative and biography, and least of all to the large number of antiquaries among them. But it must occur to historians whose work is 'problem-oriented'. They are mostly historians of society and culture, and they frequently share their interests with their next-door theoreticians – the sociologists, the economists, the philosophers. Where they differ from the theoreticians is in their reliance on the evidence of past changes. Past change is obviously the *raison d'être* of their being what they are: the main justification of an historical approach to problems as against other possible approaches. Many of them might therefore share my colleague's fears, lest by playing down historical changes we remove history itself from the work of historians.

Needless to say, the threat to history is not quite so wholesale. No historian has ever proposed, and no historian can propose, to remove all

---

[1] First published in *The Economic History Review*, Second Series, vol. XIV, no. 3, 1962.
[2] *Carte Nativorum*, ed. C. Brooke and M. Postan (Northamptonshire Record Soc. 1960).

change from every branch of history. I shall have to emphasize again and again – indeed this is one of the main propositions of this essay – that my objections to the historian's preoccupation with change relate to some fields of history and not to others. And even in these fields the historical changes which studies like mine may appear to disregard are the cumulative ones, i.e. those which historians assume to be linked in continuous sequences. These changes have, of course, always been regarded as historical *par excellence*: the ones best able to reveal the essence of the historical process. Strung out in their proper order they are supposed to exhibit that movement of evolutionary growth which used to be termed progressive, before the term became non-U. And the assumption of some such progression was until very recently to be found in every historical study of society and culture. It has inspired the various German theories of stages of development: Hildebrand's, Bücher's, Schmoller's, Sombart's. It is assumed in the various theories of the origin and diffusion of culture as expounded by the nineteenth-century sociologists and anthropologists, and especially Tylor and Spencer. It is postulated in the classical histories of legal institutions from Savigny and Puchta to Maine, Maitland, and Vinogradov; but it is in the dialectical philosophy of history, both idealist and materialist, that it has found its furthest and most articulate expression, and is now entrenched most deeply.

What are and what are not the irreducible essentials of the dialectical view of history is something about which no two pundits will agree. In official literature – in the patristic writings as well as in the synodal decrees – the core of the doctrine is now encrusted with a number of extraneous notions. I am not the right person and this is not the right occasion for an attempt to free the historical dialectic of its barnacles. Some of them, however, must be scraped away before we can recognize the main design.

That the design is not dependent on either materialism or idealism as philosophical systems is too obvious to be argued. In any case, since Lenin's day and perhaps even earlier the spokesmen of materialist dialectic have laid so great an emphasis on the political and ideological factors and have been so anxious to disassociate themselves from the crudities of simple or 'bourgeois' materialism as to blur much of the old contrast between the idealist and materialist versions of the dialectic.

Less obvious is the irrelevance of the view of history as a progression of opposites. In Hegel's own estimation this turbulent view of history was his most important invention, distinguishing him from the philosophers who viewed the historical process as one of direct and gradual emergence.

Function and dialectic in economic history

But does the historical dialectic of 1961 in fact differentiate between conflict and gradual emergence as clearly as Hegel did in 1835? It is indeed possible to argue that dialectical materialists, including Engels himself, have done their best to explain away the difference between conflict and emergence. We are all familiar with the epistemological argument of dialectical philosophers, expounded by Engels, that changes in *quality* (which is their way of describing fundamental historical transformations) are nothing else than final instalments in the continuous accretions of *quantity* (which is their way of describing gradual historical change). We are also familiar with the dialectical argument about new historical situations being born in the womb of old ones. This Marxian obstetric, if combined with Engels's epistemology, must weaken, and weaken greatly, the orthodox juxtaposition of conflict and gradual emergence: in fact it reduces it to one of words.

But even if the orthodox will not allow us to remove the doctrine of conflict from the core of the dialectic, they must join us in discarding the form in which this doctrine has been vulgarized: I mean the famous triade of thesis, antithesis, and synthesis. It is now more than fifty years since Plekhanov demonstrated, to Lenin's apparent satisfaction, how irrelevant the triade was to the essence of the dialectic. It never was anything more than a literary device, a trick of exposition. Certainly neither Engels nor Hegel ever argued that all historical transformations necessarily passed through three phases and not through four, five, or two.

What is then the essential residue of the historical dialectic? I believe it will be found in exclusive preoccupation with linked historical sequences. A dialectical explanation of an historical situation will demonstrate how it arose from the situation which preceded it; a dialectical prognosis will show how a certain future is fashioned by forces operating in the present. Past, present, and future are but steps in the 'ascending ladder of necessity': a ladder in which every step is so fully supported by the step below and so fully supports the step above that its relative position between the two will tell us all we need know about itself as well as about the ladder as a whole. In other words the historical dialectic is an attitude to social and historical phenomena which seeks to explain them by their relative positions in time.

This residual essence of the historical dialectic is, of course, something much less than either the Hegelian or the Marxist philosophy of history taken in its entirety. Marxists will have every reason for protesting that their doctrine (especially in its Leninist incarnation) embraces a universe of ideas too wide to be reduced to a mere penchant for arguments from antecedents. We are not however discussing here Marxism or Hegelianism as entire philosophical or sociological systems; all that concerns us here is their dialectic attitude to history. Indeed it is possible to argue, as I shall argue later, that some of the other components of Marxist philosophy – especially its so-called materialism – may lead a consistent Marxist into attitudes which are the reverse of the dialectical. Yet in so far as the Marxist operates as a practitioner of the historical dialectic, what he hopes to find in history is not the contemporaneous relations between material bases and their various superstructures, but the causal necessity of social development asserting itself through time.

This attitude to historical causality is frequently described as 'evolutionary'. The historical dialectic has undoubtedly received some of its inspiration from the evolutionary theories in biology, with which it shares its inclination to derive later phenomena from the earlier ones, as well as its obsessive preoccupation with origins. Nevertheless, I prefer not to employ this time-honoured name here. For not only is the historian's preoccupation with antecedents much older than the evolutionary theories of nineteenth-century biology, but in its dialectical form it is also different from them. It is both more comprehensive and more unilinear than the idea of evolution *per se*. It is more comprehensive in so far as it sometimes operates with universal entities. Whereas in biology the evolutionary idea is as a rule applied to individual forms of life – type, species, genus – the historian or the sociologist of the kind I have in mind is often prepared to derive from antecedents entire historical situations, or to arrange into a ladder of necessity whole systems of culture and social organization, and in doing so to describe them as 'stages' or 'phases' of their history. But he is also more exclusive in that, unlike the evolutionary biologist, he as a rule neglects the regressive phenomena of social change and is inclined not to take into account those moments in history when the direction of historical change was not forward but in reverse, or when the change was so slow and so small as not to matter.

It is because the comprehensive and exclusive versions of the evolutionary idea are so well exemplified in the dialectic that I prefer its label to the Darwinian one. The label, however, need not confine our discussion to the Marxists and the Hegelians. In the hands of the practitioners of academic history the dialectical argument may be incomparably less consistent, and is certainly less articulate than in the hands of the Marxists. Yet academic history is not any less dialectical for that. In so far as an historian thinks that he can account for a later situation by deriving it from an earlier one, he is an Hegelian – albeit an absent-minded one.

II

It would be unnecessary for me to remind the reader how tenacious has the dialectical bias proved to be. It has survived to our own day and has outlived by at least half a century the theory of progress which gave it birth. That revolutionary Marxists should cling to it is perhaps not surprising. It enables them to turn a political hope into a scientific certainty by demonstrating that socialist future must emerge from capitalist past as surely as the capitalist present has emerged from the feudal past.

But these of course are not the attractions of the dialectic for the main body of historians. Some such attraction is perhaps inherent in the very occupation of historians. What makes a fact appear historical to an historian is its preterite nature – its place in past time. What can then be more natural than to assume that its position in past time is sufficient not only to locate an historical fact but also to explain it? The argument that *post hoc* is *propter hoc* comes naturally to historians. It is one of their professional proclivities, their occupational deportment.

Yet I doubt whether even this proclivity, common as it is, would have dominated the study of history had it not offered certain obvious working conveniences. The convenience of which historians avail themselves most readily is that of being able to fill gaps in historical exposition by a procedure which the statisticians would describe as one of interpolation, i.e. by making up for what they know they do not know about one period by deductions from what they think they know about another period. As long as the historian takes it for granted that society, with all its activities, arts and artefacts, grew from epoch to epoch, what is there to prevent him from concluding, as Herbert Spencer did, that everything in the past was smaller and simpler than in the early nineteenth century, and that the nearer humanity got to the Victorian age, the bigger, the better, the more highly differentiated and the more highly co-ordinated everything became?

To historians, especially the social and economic ones, these con- clusions offer a convenience of inestimable value. By assuming that every social situation of which they have no knowledge is intermediate to an anterior and posterior situation they think they know, historians have been able to pass innumerable verdicts without having to bother about the evidence. Although they knew next to nothing about population before 1801, and least of all about population between the thirteenth century and the end of the seventeenth, they were, until recently, telling countless generations of readers and students that all through the seventeenth century population continued the demographic growth of the sixteenth, and that the population of the fifteenth century was greater than that of the thirteenth. Although little is known about the actual volume of trade in the Middle Ages, the historians have gone on writing about the trade of the fifteenth century as if it was greater in volume than that of, say, the thirteenth, and of the trade of the twelfth century as if it was unquestionably smaller and more restricted than that of the fourteenth century. By a similar process of interpolation historians were able to represent the English economic record of the last thirty years before 1914 as a continuation of the great mid-Victorian achievement.

III

I have cited these particular intances of dialectical interpolation because they mark the points at which the dialectic has now ceased to be of practical convenience in my own work. It is largely because at a number of important points the dialectic interpolations have failed to survive the test of evidence that some economic historians now question the usefulness of the dialectic itself. If population did not expand continually through all the centuries of English history; if trade did not grow all the time in scale and complexity; if productive capital was not constantly accumulating through centuries; if inequalities of wealth and social differences based on them were not necessarily smaller in the earlier centuries than in the latter, of what help can the dialectic be to the interpolating historian?

The damage which recent work has inflicted on the dialectic is not, however, confined to the doubts it cast on the uses of interpolation. The main historical structure of the dialectic, its very chain of progression, has been made unsafe by what historians have lately done to some of its rungs. The phases of pre-feudal communism, slavery, feudalism, early capitalism, industrial capitalism, could all be arranged in a series only as long as their historical quantities were thought to be equivalent. They were, of course, all different – that goes without saying – but differences between them were assumed to be equally profound. It was only because the differences were equally profound that it was possible to represent the passage from one phase to another as a real turning point, and to represent all history as a sequence, or if you wish, a cotillon, of turning points. This is now rapidly becoming impossible. The turning points hitherto chosen to mark stages in dialectic progression no longer appear to be sufficiently equivalent to be arranged in a significant series.

This new difficulty has been created largely by studies of industrialization. As a result of the recent interest in economic growth, historians have been occupying themselves more than ever before with industrial revolutions and especially with the Industrial Revolution in England. The consequent repercussions in other fields of economic history have been, or at least should be, far-reaching. For a long time the tendency among historians of the English Industrial Revolution has been to argue that it did not come in 1760 and did not end in 1815; that its precursory movements had started generations before the middle of the eighteenth century, that it was still in full flood at the height of the Victorian era. This is still the prevailing view of historians on the dates of the Industrial Revolution. In recent years, however, the attention of historians has been drawn not only to the chronology or the duration of the revolution, but also to its size. That the revolution was a protracted process is not now questioned; but, for all its gradualness, it now appears to historians as more cataclysmic than any other economic and social change in all the centuries of medieval and post-medieval history. The cataclysmic view of the Industrial Revolution does not depend on whether there was a true explosion of economic activity – a 'take off' following a long period of preparatory 'run up'. Even if some economic historians continue to believe that the movement of industrialization proceeded at about the same pace throughout its history, they would still be unable to deny that the cumulative effects of the transformation were more profound and more irrevocable than any other economic transformation since the end of the Roman Empire. Europe, and with her the world, was never the same again.

If this view of the Industrial Revolution is right, it is bound to modify our attitude to historical changes on both sides of the divide, and more especially to changes on its pre-industrial side. Viewed through the screen of the Industrial Revolution, the centuries of pre-industrial history must now appear very placid. The placidity of the pre-industrial epoch may of course be an optical illusion. Movements within it were many and profound; but as we now realize, not all the movements were forward and not all the forward movements were cumulative. Compared with the great forward leap of the Industrial Revolution, movements which were not only smaller in scale, but also neither forward nor cumulative are bound to appear as mere shuffles. And shuffles are not what the great transformations of the dialectical process are made of, and not what historical interpolations can be derived from.

It is therefore no wonder that at least one continental text-book of economic and social history carries the story of the Middle Ages to the end of the eighteenth century, and that in certain fashionable disputations on the periodization of history the tendency has been to push the turning point between the middle and the modern ages ever nearer to the eighteenth century.

IV

This revaluation of the Industrial Revolution has a number of other implications, historical and sociological, which need not concern us here. We are concerned only with the damage it has inflicted on the dialectic, especially the absent-minded dialectic of non-Marxist history. Yet what is important is not that the absent-minded dialectic should have been discomfited but that its discomfiture should have produced so little discomfort. Historical study has not suffered from it; historians themselves may not have even noticed it. The truth of the matter is that for all the dialectical and evolutionary bias of historians, preoccupation with dialectical change is not as essential to the health of historical study as it might at first sight appear. Had the sole business of history been to trace the working of recent cumulative evolution, the damage inflicted on the dialectic might have damaged history itself. If recent work of historians has not had this effect, it is because the claims of history to an intellectual status do not rest on its liaison with consecutive change. Even if we must abandon the search for cumulative transformations, we can still busy ourselves with other tasks, or at least one other task. We may be unable to explain our phenomena merely by showing how they followed similar phenomena of an earlier age; but we still can show how they fitted into other phenomena of the same age. And this weaving of some historical facts with other historical facts into a cloth of an epoch may in some fields of study do more for our understanding of mankind than the spinning of facts with their antecedents into evolutionary yarns.

This is an attitude which sociologists, and more especially the social anthropologists, will recognize as their own. Before the last war they would have decorated it with the title of 'functional'. The decoration is no longer worn as proudly and on as many occasions as it used to be, but the attitude it advertises is, as Professor Fortes has recently reminded us, the professional stance of anthropology. Social function and social structure are the sociologists' main tools of analysis, or as they would themselves prefer to put it, their main heuristic concepts. The sociologist would try to relate the institution and the activity he is studying to the other institutions and activities in the same society, or, if I am allowed a somewhat question-begging form of words, he would try to 'explain' them by their social functions.

42

Function and dialectic in economic history

Needless to say the meaning of the word function, like all meanings of all words, and more especially of academic words, is very imprecise. This imprecision is something we have not yet learned to live with, but sociologists are perhaps more worried about their vocabulary than the practitioners in other fields of study are about theirs. And in their mood of terminological hypochondria they have been telling each other and the world in general about the multiple connotation of the term function. I do not propose to follow them through all the thousand and one senses in which the word can be and has been used. But two of these senses reveal an ambiguity so fundamental, and yet from our point of view so fortunate, as to deserve some attention even from the happy-go-lucky historians.

The ambiguity I have in mind is the one which sociologists noticed almost as soon as they began using the term; in fact it is the one which Radcliffe Brown, one of the fathers of functional sociology, was the first to point out. The word function is most commonly used either in its biological sense or its algebraic one. Durkheim, from whom modern sociology derives so many of its ideas, gave currency to the concept of function in its biological variant: he wrote about the correspondence between social phenomena and the needs of the social organism. This sense is still implied even when sociologists do their best to eschew such alien notions as organism or such teleological ideas as needs. In one of Radcliffe Brown's formulations function is a 'contribution which a partial activity makes to a total activity of which it is a part'. The formula is very aseptic but clearly and avowedly biological.

In its algebraic sense the term function has been used since Euler first introduced it in the eighteenth century to designate pairs of co-variables, i.e. phenomena so linked in operation that a change in one will produce a related change in the other. I believe it is largely in this sense that the concept is employed in some anthropological studies of myth and kinship, or in anthropologically minded studies of ancient religions.

This is the major ambiguity of function. But worrying as it may be to anthropologists, it is something of a godsend to historians in that it not only enjoins them to interpret historical phenomena by their place in contemporary contexts, but also implies that the place of a phenomenon in its social context is sometimes best revealed by the manner of its change.

To us historians this implication is highly important, for it draws our attention to historical change and at the same time helps us to distinguish the relevant aspects of change from the irrelevant ones. After all, the main fault of the dialectical answers to historical problems is not their error of fact but their irrelevance in argument. The retort proper to them is not 'sez you' but 'so what?'. Even when a dialectical or evolutionary demonstration appears to be right, i.e. well supported by evidence, as some of them are, it may still fail to explain anything. Medieval serfdom may have descended from Roman slavery, but how does this help us to understand it? The case against this particular form of academic irrelevance is the same as that which sociologists and anthropologists used to advance against the so-called diffusionist schools of ethnology. Even if it could be proved that an institution was handed down from one society to another or from an earlier age to a later one, it would still remain to be discovered why other societies, or other ages, took it over. That they in fact did so, often means that they had a use for it, or in other words, that it had a social function to perform. The function of an institution or a technique or an idea in its new environment may not necessarily be the one it performed in the old. Indeed, if the new environment is no longer the same, it is difficult to imagine how all its bits and pieces taken over from a different age could have preserved intact their erstwhile functions or their old forms.

The transfer of an institution from century to century, and for that matter from place to place, is therefore a process of change. It is not, or rather not always, continuous and cumulative, but it is invariably a process in which society as a whole and individual phenomena within it are linked as functional co-variants. And as long as they are so linked the student may find in them the key he is looking for: the key both to the historical phenomenon in which he happens to be interested and to the social system to which the phenomenon happens to belong.

V

It is because the term function is sufficiently ambiguous to be employed not only in its biological sense, but also in its mathematical or dynamic connotation, that I find it so useful in defining an attitude which is not evolutionary, but truly and profoundly historical. An historian must concern himself with change, because change illuminates as nothing else can the nature of social problems; but light thus shed comes not only from the direct current running through the unbroken continuum of history, but also from those alternating impulses by means of which ideas or institutions adjust themselves to the shifting historical environments.

Thus, even though medievalists may find it impossible to discover the time or the place in which trade first originated or money was unknown, and even though they may doubt whether trade or currency or credit or economic equality or social differences grew from century to century, they have not thereby removed history from medieval study. For as long as trade or currency or anything else altered in volume or importance or form from one period to another, the need to understand that alteration may take historians at least as deeply into the mystery of mankind as any other form of historical inquiry.

This is my prescription for Dr N's fears. I must, however, make it clear that it is not a brand new medicine and still less a universal cure. The advice to fit facts into their epoch may to most working historians appear obvious and familiar. Is this not what most historians now in fact do? And does this not in fact represent the attitude of that most plodding of historians who disclaims all interest outside his 'own period'? Nevertheless, the advice is not wholly superfluous. Confinement to a narrow patch does not necessarily protect one from illusions about the world outside it. Very often historians who disclaim all knowledge of other periods hold unconscious beliefs about them which colour their view of 'their own' period. Does not Kosminsky, in spite of his repeated protests that all he is concerned with is the thirteenth century, pepper his book with 'not yets' and 'alreadys', which betray some very firm ideas as to what happened before and after his chosen century? Of these ideas Kosminsky himself is very conscious and even proud, for they are all derived from the Marxist doctrine. No doubt other historians may often honestly try to keep within the bounds of their chosen century or reign. But it is precisely among these time-bound historians that we find the most incurable strayers into other periods: incurable because their strayings are so somnambulistic.

However, the academic scholar confined to 'his period' is not the only brand of historian to bear an artificial resemblance to a functional sociologist. The Marxists when dealing with the history of ideas, beliefs, art or legal doctrine, will often try to demonstrate how these elements of culture derive from contemporaneous economic phenomena, or to use their own terminology, from the 'social relations of production'. In doing so they will occupy themselves with lateral links and not with roots in the past, with concomitants rather than with antecedents. And as this is what Marxists have been doing from the earliest days, whole generations in advance of Durkheim or Weber, they might well claim to have discovered the functional medicine long before economic historians like myself ever thought of prescribing it.

This, I believe, would be a vain claim: vain for at least two reasons. To begin with, not all lateral connections make up into a functional pre-scription. A sociologically-minded historian confronted with an economic phenomenon would try to fit it into the totality of contemporary society and culture: this would be an historical interpretation of the economy. A Marxian materialist would do the very opposite. He would try to fit the totality of society and culture to a single phenomenon – the one he assumes to be 'basic'. He would in other words try and account for entire historical situations by economic facts within them. This may be well worth doing, but it is not economic or social history, it is economic interpretation of history. Its argument may be lateral and concomitant, but it is the very inversion of functional.

The second reason why I think the claim is vain is one of credentials. Much as a dialectical materialist would insist on the indissoluble fusion of his materialism and his dialectic, the two are clearly distinguishable and separable constituents of the Marxist ideology – its two faces. In judging a demonstration of Marxian methods in historical study it is therefore important to make sure which of the faces is on view. When a Marxist demonstrates how free capitalist farming derived from villeinage and how the latter derived from slavery he brings his dialectic into play, but when he demonstrates how feudal law, politics, society, and literature derived from manorial economy, he performs as a materialist and must be judged as such.

This distinction is most germane to our inquiry. Does it matter, you will ask, under what credentials, in what role we approach the truth, provided we approach it? I believe that the role matters a great deal. Because they have approached the problem as materialists the Marxists have chosen for treatment by concomitant correlation the very aspects of history which are least suited to it.

This brings us to the main point of our argument: the one with which I have started and with which I am going to conclude. In summarizing the functional prescription for Dr N's fears I disclaimed all pretensions to a universal panacea. Function is as good as, or better than, the dialectic in some applications; not necessarily in all. Throughout this essay I have referred to what some historians might do or ought to do in their own fields of study, not to what all historians can and will do whenever history is studied. I have chosen most of my examples from economic and social history. This I have done not only because these happen to be subjects of which I am least ignorant, but because I believe that they belong to a field of history to which function provides a better key than the dialectic. Subjects in some other fields of historical study can be well or even better illuminated not by relating them to their contemporary setting, but by confronting them with their own antecedents. If, for the sake of argument, we divide the various branches of history in the same way in which history is departmentalized for the purpose of teaching and research, and distinguish economic and social history from the history of ideas or science, religion or philosophy, the proportions in which functions and dialectic must be prescribed will differ from branch to branch. It so happens that the branches of history concerned with what Marxists would call the material basis, i.e. with economic activity and the attendant social relations, happens to be the ones least suited to dialectical treatment and best served by functional analysis. But as we approach regions of ideas and techniques, i.e. regions in which achievements of one generation are deposited for use by other generations, and in which men learn from the lessons of their predecessors, or else react against them, the dialectic may do more or at least as much to explain the course of historical change as function.

It is for this reason that the credentials under which Marxists appear in what may seem to be functional performances, prevent us from accepting them in that role. The trouble about the dialectic is not that it is wholly inapplicable to history, but that it is so frequently applied to fields in which it happens to be least useful. If function and dialectic are to be reconciled and allowed their proper place in historical work, it will perhaps be necessary to move a stage beyond the philosophical position which Marx took up in the 1840s. Having put the dialectic on its head, and made it materialist, Marx has directed it into regions to which this posture is unsuited. If we complete the somersault and put the dialectic on its feet again, we might thereby return it to where it belongs.[1]

[1] However, in a recent paper to the Economic History Society at their meeting in Durham in 1969, Dr A. Wrigley drew attention to a branch of 'material' history, i.e. that of population, to which what I consider the dialectical method is highly appropriate, since death rates, frequencies and fertilities of marriage in one generation profoundly affect the demographic situation in subsequent generations.

5

FACT AND RELEVANCE IN
HISTORICAL STUDY[1]

I

Most orthodox historians cling to the belief that their real business is to study facts. The belief testifies to the modesty of their ambitions, but it also betrays some lack of intellectual sophistication, for only men innocent of philosophy will confine the object of historical study to facts, as historians conceive them.

'As historians conceive them.' The historians' conception of what historical facts are is not easy to get hold of. In keeping with the traditional unselfconsciousness of their profession, most historians prefer to be unaware of their epistemology. Nevertheless, a critic observing his fellow-historians at close quarters should not find it impossible to lay bare the conception, or rather the several conceptions composing their view of their facts.

In this composition the ingredient most intimately involved with epistemological issues also happens to be the one historians share with workers in many other fields. Whether they realize it or not, historians devoted to 'facts as they were' accept by implication the fundamental postulates of philosophical realism. They must presuppose that human knowledge directly corresponds to the objective reality of the world, the *Dinge an sich*, and can faithfully reproduce it. On this issue their proper alignment should be with the anti-idealists and anti-subjectivists. Outsiders may therefore think it odd that on other fundamental issues the historians most conscious of their allegiance to factual history should be so frequently found siding with the idealist metaphysicians, Hegel, Kant, Rickert, or Dilthey. But then outsiders do not know their historians. Such are the blessings of philosophical absent-mindedness that many historians find it only too easy to avow their allegiance to philosophical idealism, while conducting their own studies on the simplest realist assumptions.

[1] First published in *Historical Studies*, vol. 13, no. 51, October 1968, University of Melbourne.

Fact and relevance in historical study

However, these, so to speak, macrophilosophical assumptions are not characteristic of historians as such and do not mark off the occupation of historians from other intellectual pursuits. Some philosophical realism is built, as it must be, into all empirical study, or indeed into all search for explanation. In their argument against subjective or solipsistic theories of knowledge philosophical realists have always been able to take their stand on the obvious proposition that all intellectual proof, including that of subjectivism itself, must in the last resort rest on postulates which are real, i.e. non-personal and non-subjective. So, however much we may regret the unconscious manner in which fact-oriented historians hold on to their realist bias, the bias itself is unexceptional and unexceptionable.

What, in the current connotation of historical fact, are exceptionable and more truly typical of the historians' professional point of view are some of the other, less general and less overtly philosophical pre-suppositions. And of the latter, none is more typical than the view of the historical past as a finite universe of facts contained within fixed and permanent frontiers.

In current discussion, the implication of the finite universe of facts appears in a variety of guises. It reveals itself most commonly in the ambition of historians to 'know all the facts'. With this ambition goes the reluctance – reluctance often taken to be the hall-mark of true scholarship – to form conclusions before 'all the facts are known'. The assumption of finite historical experience also inspires the fashionable case for general history defined as 'history in all its aspects'.

Of all these guises, the one deserving the best attention of critics is that of 'general history', if only because it happens to be fashionable at the moment. The inspiration behind it is often purely negative: the dislike of sectoral specialization, whether economic, social, legal or intellectual. But, as a rule, the advocates of general history are also able to invoke positive reasons. Historians discussing history are never more positive or plausible than when they try to remind us of the indivisible substance of the historical process, or when they plead that individual institutions and activities should always be considered in the functional and structural setting of society as a whole.

Indeed so plausible, as well as fashionable, is the case for general history that to argue, as I shall do later, in defence of sectoral specialization may at first sight appear unreasonable to the point of perversity. But I trust that the average historian, be he never so orthodox, will not think it wholly unreasonable of me to argue that general history is unattainable, or at least impractical, even if it were desirable.

Fact and relevance

What makes general history unattainable is the sheer immensity of past experience. The hope that history can reconstruct the past in all its aspects as a single story assumes that the universe of social experience is intellectually exhaustible. Some historians hope to exhaust it merely by dipping into it; writers of textbooks of general history think they fulfil their assignment by tacking on to a story of politics a few postscripts on the economy, on art, on science or on any other aspect of the past which happens to have been studied by historians. What such aspirants to general history do not as a rule acknowledge is how much wider is the spectrum of past experience than the combined area of all its bands which have so far hit the historian's eye.

The range of the historian's vision has, of course, been constantly widening. Before the late eighteenth century – or the seventeenth in England – European historiography had been largely confined to wars, politics and the affairs of the church. Since then several other fields have been added to the historian's territory: law, constitutions, economic policy, social structure, scientific discovery, philosophical and scientific activity; and there is no knowing what further areas of the past will before long be brought within the historians' horizon in response to the shifting interests of the world at large. Yet, however widely will historians have broadened their field of vision, they will not thereby have acquired a general view of the historical process. A more general view perhaps; and we must not be so ungenerous as not to admit that for some purposes, mainly those of school-teaching, more general histories, be they a mere hotch-potch of separate sectoral stories, could be more satisfactory than the more specialized ones. But this degree of generality and this limited usefulness is all the writers of general history can hope for. Their scope will always be confined to those few aspects of the past which for various reasons happen to have swum into the historians' net. The notion that these aspects can in combination cover the totality of past experience and reveal to our view the 'social process in its entirety' or the 'historical change in all its manifestations' is one of the characteristic intellectual delusions of historians as a profession.

The reason why this particular delusion has been singled out is that it represents at its clearest and its most vulnerable the attitudes of historians who wish to confine themselves to mere discovery of facts. These attitudes, especially the reticences which hold back the 'pure' scholar from drawing conclusions until 'all the facts are known', are understandable and even commendable. There is everything to be said for the implied caveat to students of historical situations about which premature conclusions have been drawn and which could be better understood if and when more fully studied.

But when applied to historical study as a whole, the determination to wait until all the facts are known conjures up a vision of the historical past which is both illusory and, in the end, hopeless. By refusing to pitch camp until they have reached the ultimate frontier of knowable facts historians merely condemn themselves to an eternity in the wilderness with the promised land of final and definitive history receding ever further away. They exile themselves to the same intellectual desert as the historians in quest of general history, and for the same reasons.

II

The argument that in the aggregate the universe of historical facts is infinite is in the last resort a quantitative one and is therefore simple to the point of truism. Moreover, in the context in which I have set it, it may also appear to be somewhat out of place. I have linked it to the successive shifts in historians' interests; but these shifts will reveal themselves more significantly not in historical experience taken as a whole, but in historical facts taken individually. Thus taken, individual historical facts – their contents and their frontiers – will turn out to be infinitely changeable and, in their changes, highly responsive to the interests of the historians themselves. For the facts of history, even those which in historical parlance figure as 'hard and fast', are no more than relevances: facets of past phenomena which happen to relate to the pre-occupations of historical inquirers at the time of their inquiries.

Every historical fact is a product of abstraction, or of the historian's limited vision. If an historical 'event' can be defined as a past occurrence, or in other words as a 'real' segment in the continuum of historical experience, then an historical fact is nothing more than one of the event's observed aspects. What makes it observable is its affinity to an interest uppermost in the observer's mind. This affinity impels the historian to focus his vision upon it; but to be able to focus the historian must also be prepared to neglect. Outside the facets of events within his focus, there must be other facets which he does not wish to observe, or even facets so far outside the range of his professional vision as to be altogether outside the scope of historical study.

The non-finite composition of historical events and the unstable succession of their facets visible to historians are both exemplified by the history of history itself. In the last two centuries successive generations of historians have discovered wholly new aspects in the most familiar historical events. In the 1960s the historians' approaches to the Norman Conquest or the Wars of the Roses or, to be more precise, the facts they have sought and discovered are not those sought and discovered by historians writing in the 1890s. The interests and the corresponding facts which nowadays occupy historians of the French Revolution are not those which drew the attention and filled the pages of a Guizot or a Thiers. Since Stalin's time and largely under his personal influence Russian histories of Ivan the Terrible and his *Oprichina* or Peter the Great have been asking questions and bringing up facts which were either absent or submerged in the older Russian histories. And even in the more specialized and theory-oriented fields of economic history, the students of medieval agrarian history, of the economic policies of the Tudor and Stuart kings, of the Industrial Revolution, or of the Great Depression – all of them well-worn topics – will now be found discovering and debating facts whose significance and whose very existence were not realized by economic historians of an earlier generation. Students of history could cite innumerable other branches of history whose complement of facts was renewed every time a new problem emerged or a new question was asked.

This is what I mean by asserting that historical facts are relevances. If this assertion is right, much of what some philosophers have been telling us about the relativity of historical facts may in a certain sense be less paradoxical than it at first appears. However real the substance of historical knowledge, the facets of reality of which this knowledge is made up, and above all the reasons why particular facets have entered historical knowledge, are all relative to the intellectual stance of the historian himself. They are all answers to his inquiries; they had not been perceived and had not been perceivable until they were lit up by the searchlight of his queries.

III

To the average working historian the process whereby he perceives and brings out, or to use his professional language, 'establishes' his facts may appear quite different. The most orthodox of academic historians might admit that his facts are established by historical study and can in this sense be said not to have existed until discovered. He would, however, insist that the process of discovery, its objects and its products, depend not on his own interests, but on those attributes of the facts themselves which make some of them more discoverable than others.

Needless to say, the attribute to which an historian would attach most importance would be that of evidence. What enables the historian to establish his facts, indeed to know that there are facts to be established, is the testimony of his sources. To an historian so minded, history is a corpus of facts which have come to his knowledge because they happen to be knowable, or in other words, have been well-served by accessible evidence.

If this point of view appears to conflict with the one I have tried to expound, the conflict can partly be put down to the historians' characteristic lack of introspection. Had they been better aware of their own procedures they might not perhaps have taken so readily for granted the alleged independence of their evidence. In so far as they are at all aware of its logical nature, they regard it as 'given' and 'pre-existent', a reservoir of ready testimony formed independently of the historian's intentions and interests, and always available for him to tap. Critical students of historiography will not, however, find it difficult to cite numerous historical studies based on evidence they had themselves called forth. In my own field, that of economic history and especially in that of medieval agrarian history, new evidence appears as new points of view emerge. Many a court roll or charter or bailiff's account, or entry in the records of royal courts now provide historians with evidence which even Maitland and Vinogradov did not use, and whose existence they may not even have suspected. Who in the 1890s knew, or wished to know, that court rolls were packed with demographic data? That charters could help in the study of capital formation? That the entries of expenses in bailiffs' accounts contained information on soil physiology and climatic fluctuations? In short, the shifting interests of historians have affected not only the choice of historical facts, but also brought into existence an ever-changing flow of evidence to serve them.

The historian-made origin of some of the testimony is not, however, the sole reason why we must not identify facts with their evidence. Some such identification can perhaps be reconciled with problem-oriented history. An historian bent on compromise may find it in a definition of facts as aspects of the past sufficiently relevant to be worth studying, and at the same time well enough provided with evidence to be capable of being established. The trouble about this compromise is that it conceals, without bridging, one of the deepest rifts in the historical camp.

The rift runs right across the present range of historical research and teaching and demarcates the two distinct areas of study commonly regarded as historical: that of antiquarian information, and that of historical fact. The fissure is not the same as that between the alternative definitions of facts and evidence, but, looked at more closely, the two lines will be found to run parallel. When historians insist on defining their facts not as relevances to their interests, but as nuggets of reality embedded in their evidence, they do so because they have been taught to identify the area of historical facts with that of established knowledge of the past.

Yet the two areas differ both in extent and location. The area of historical facts comprises the entire universe of historical discourse. By definition it must be wider than the field of established historical knowledge for it must contain not only facts established by the full test of evidence and also those in the process of being established, but also facts for which the evidence is not sufficient to make them fully and finally establishable. It may even contain those near-facts which for lack of sources may never emerge from their chrysalis stage of conjecture. By comparison, the field of established knowledge is not only much narrower, but is also to some extent extraneous, since some of its acres must of necessity lie outside the boundaries of historical discourse. For included within it we shall find pieces or even areas of information commonly accepted as historical, yet not relevant to any live interest or problem, political, social or philosophical. To historians who link their facts to problems, all particles of knowledge not so linked must appear as non-facts, and the body of knowledge comprising them as non-history.

This must not be taken to mean that information unrelated to problems is wholly worthless wasteland. For all its lack of intellectual content it may attract the man in the street, and do so better than the intellectual fare served to him by the problem-oriented historians. Some of it will attract by its appearance of antiquity, by the imprint of past centuries and by the beauty of the patina. Other pieces of information may possess the allurements of mere oddity, and amuse by their contrast to similar objects of more recent date. When such pieces of information are described as 'antiquarian' this description need not be taken in a derogatory sense. Activities capable of diverting may for this reason alone deserve their favour with the public and their support by the state.

Much harder to defend are the areas of reputedly historical knowledge made up of ex-facts. Ex-facts are pieces of knowledge relevant to problems which were alive once upon a time, but have expired by now. Text books of history and history curricula in schools and universities are loaded with ex-facts which have lost their relevance without acquiring the allurements of the antique and the picturesque. They neither enlighten nor divert, yet they occupy a great deal of space in the field of accepted and recommended historical knowledge. Much of what now passes for constitutional history, especially that of the Middle Ages or the sixteenth century, is made up of topics which had been quick with life a hundred or a hundred and fifty years ago, but died long before the present century began. The topics may still have some necromantic attraction to the historians of history, and may still be worth preserving in the sacred memory of past preoccupations. But the main reason why they have survived the age which bore them is the embalming action of text books and examinations. The machinery of academic curricula moves so slowly, if it moves at all, that it makes it difficult to clear the academic teaching of its corpses. Their continued use in schools and universities is sometimes justified by the technical training they can provide to beginners. The obvious parallel is that of anatomical dissection. The assumption is that the technical arts of historical investigation could not be taught on live historical problems; whereas in reality historical technology taught not in dissecting theatres but in life classes might instruct pupils not only in the handling of the evidence but also in the art of historical relevance.

IV

What makes the art of historical relevance teachable is that its places of instruction – the professional and social positions from which it can best be learned – are several and all open to choice. One or two of the positions are sited in the very midst of the public concourse, and could be occupied without any preparation or planning on the historian's part. Others have been deliberately mapped out to fit the special needs of historians.

Of the different sites, the most open and the least planned ones are those directly exposed to the intellectual and political winds. Once upon a time, historians responded to the prevailing winds not only easily but also usefully, or at least as usefully as was expected of them. In the heroic days of European historiography at the beginning of the nineteenth century they assumed the role of intellectual windmills and busily ground away at the grist fed to them by the public at large. At that time the European intelligentsia, disillusioned with rationalist *philosophes* of the eighteenth century, turned to history for lessons. The law reformers, and still more, the defenders of the legal systems, recoiled from Montesquieu, or from what they believed Montesquieu stood for; legal historians like Savigny and Puchta responded by trying to derive wisdom about laws from their past development. Constitutional historians, from Gneist onwards, similarly met the demand for a doctrine of government derived from history. At about the same time a whole succession of social historians, from Möser and Nitzsch in Germany, to Fustel de Coulanges in France and to Kliuchevsky in Russia, tried to lay bare the historical roots of serfdom and thereby to demonstrate how shallow they ran and how easy they were to cut. Somewhat later still the economic historians who represented themselves as the economists of the historical school, such as List or Schmoller in Germany, or Cunningham in England, tried to counter the teaching of Adam Smith and Ricardo and its free-trade message by lessons drawn from the historical record of medieval and mercantilist governments.

From the point of view of statesmen and philosophers and certainly from that of the world's eventual benefit, some of these historical lessons may not have been worth taking. Some of them may even have done a good deal of harm. But from the point of view of historical study itself their effect was wholly to the good. New themes of historical jurisprudence and historical economics entered the scope of the historical interests and made up a new complement of ideas which for generations to come were to provide professional historians with their stock-in-trade.

Nowadays the historians as a profession do not expose themselves to the challenge of contemporary politics or philosophical debate as openly and as fully as they did a century ago. For one thing, politicians or ordinary educated people no longer look to history for lessons. Yet in spite of all the public indifference to historical lessons, and in spite of all the reluctance of professional historians to draw them, some individual historians still involve themselves and their professional activities with contemporary events. Men like R. H. Tawney participated fully in contemporary politics and social movements and, in doing so, infused their historical work with relevances to the problems of the day. Tawney was, of course, capable of thought and action beyond the means of smaller men. But whatever the latters' stature it need not prevent them from sharing in the preoccupations of their contemporaries and from tying up their share in the world with their work as historians.

Such participation may not be to every historian's taste, since many historians choose their scholarly vocation with the express purpose of loosening their ties with the world they live in. In Tawney's words, 'they make a little darkness and call it research'. This predilection for little darknesses need not, however, be accepted as the historians' universal rule of conduct, for historians who do not follow it are still to be found in some numbers.

If their numbers are not larger than they are, this is partly because to historians the involvement with contemporary affairs cannot be wholly painless. Historians who live wholly in their world and also weave their scholarly activities into the fabric of their mundane lives must both suffer and benefit therefrom. But whatever may happen to be the balance of profit and loss for individual historians, the profession as a whole has always gained, and will continue to gain from the involvement.

Individual historians may, however, find the exposure to the world and its problems less painful and more in keeping with their professional predilections if and when it comes through their study of contemporary history. Its benefits need not be confined to students wholly occupied with the history of their own time; some benefits will accrue even to historians taking smaller doses of contemporary themes in addition to such other history as happens to occupy their main attention. These supplementary doses are not frequently prescribed, but they do not appear to have done harm to the men who have taken them. When, as a beginner, I told Tawney of my decision to concentrate on the later Middle Ages, his advice to me was to engage in some very modern history as well – 'it would keep you in touch'. He himself both read and taught some recent history in addition to his work on the sixteenth and seventeenth centuries. I believe that he also encouraged Eileen Power to keep up her historical interest in the modern Far East. Most of the historians who helped in the writing of the civil histories of the War have not thereby lost all their worth in the fields of historical study they normally cultivate. Their editor-in-chief, Sir Keith Hancock, is, of course, a contemporary historian *par excellence*.

The pursuit of contemporary history, like the direct exposure to the prevailing winds, cannot be wholly costless. Contemporary historians must frequently make do with evidence which is necessarily incomplete and is also too fresh from the oven to be easily digested. The verdicts based on it must therefore be more transitory than scholarly verdicts usually are. The contemporary historian's own position imposes yet additional costs. He is, as a rule, a participant in the events he describes, their victim or their beneficiary, or at least their direct witness. He cannot therefore judge them with the detachment expected from an historian.

The costs are, however, reimbursable. Practitioners of contemporary history may incur higher professional risks than the students of older and safer periods. But unlike so many of the latter, they are able to infuse their work with the relevance and even urgency out of other students' reach. It is however the historians in the aggregate and historical study *in toto* who benefit from the infusion most. In the long run they are the contemporary historians' residuary legatees.

V

It is nevertheless doubtful whether the safest access to contemporary relevances necessarily lies in the two open situations I have so far located. I have already suggested that for some individual historians – as distinct from historical study *in toto* – the penalties of involving themselves and their studies with contemporary interests, or even with complementary studies of contemporary history, may prove to be too great to be worth incurring. They may find safer, though technically more difficult, points of access to new relevances on sites appropriated and developed by others, but available to willing sharers. In other words, instead of trying to absorb new interests, so to speak, in the raw, by participating in current affairs or by chronicling contemporary events, historians may prefer to receive them mediatized – and thereby also refined and intellectualized – from philosophy and social science.

This has always been one of historians' several ways of exposing themselves to outside stimuli. From time to time the historian and the social scientist have usefully invaded each other's preserves. Since the earliest days of modern historiography historians have been able to enrich their stock of topics and interests either by raiding the neighbouring areas of political and social theory, or by opening their own gates to invading theoreticians. In the early nineteenth century historians formed themselves into marauding bands – the so-called 'historical schools' of jurisprudence, politics and economics – with the avowed object of annexing the neighbouring fields of political and social science. The reciprocal incursions from theory to history are even older. By their very use of historical examples, political philosophers, from Machiavelli to Graham Wallas, entered the field of historical study and left behind masses of intellectual ammunition which historians still go on firing.

Some such mutual raiding goes on in our own day; it may even have been provoked by certain recent developments. A friendly observer of modern sociology will not fail to notice the growing inclination on the part of sociologists – an inclination hitherto restricted to Marxists – to cast their studies on an extended time-scale, and consequently to use historical materials and to produce near-historical results. The same tendency has revealed itself more clearly in modern economics and econometrics. As a result of their pre-occupation with economic development, the present generation of economists have turned their attention to the why and the how of past growth. Econometric assessment of past national incomes, or of their allocation to factors, and the attempts to

Fact and relevance in historical study

define and to measure the various 'inputs' into past economic growth, have generated a succession of studies, theoretical in form and language, but historical in substance. These studies have already influenced the writing and teaching of history and have imported new interests and topics into it; and the importation shows every sign of speeding up.

In recent times the inter-disciplinary raids initiated by historians have been occurring even more frequently than the invasions of their field by non-historians. They have certainly been sufficiently frequent to disturb the contents of modern historiography. Much of the current work on the structure of politics, especially that on the social bases of political parties, has been done by historians, round the problems and concepts taken over from political sociology. The take-over may be partly to blame for some of the shortcomings of the socio-political histories. If their conceptual wherewithal sometimes appears to be vague and loosely assembled, the fault probably lies with the political sociologists. The latter have not yet fashioned a system of concepts sufficiently firm and clear to be borrowed for use by mere historians.

Where such systems exist and are generally accepted, as in economics, the historians have been able to borrow and to invest them profitably. Studies by both economists and historians, such as those of foreign trade and tariffs by Jacob Viner or those of international payments by Jenks, Feis, or White, or those of fluctuations and cycles by Matthews and Rostow, or those of industrialization and technological change by Habakkuk and Ashton, have all made their contribution to both history and economics. Most of them, in addition to illustrating or accounting for certain historical situations, have also exemplified and thereby helped to establish certain important propositions of economic theory. But what from our point of view here is most important is their success in infecting the main body of economic history with new problems and arguments.

The contagion of historical study, above all that of economic history, by social sciences, may still be no more than endemic. It matters not that in some cases it may have so far remained skin deep and has not entered the bloodstream of historical thought. One such case of superficial contagion is perhaps that of the so-called 'new economic history'. The main ambition of the new economic historians has been to bring the mathematical techniques of econometrics to bear upon such topics of American history as the emancipation of the slaves, the contribution of railways to American progress, or the banking crisis of the nineteenth century. The studies so far carried out have amply proved that the mathematical tools of modern economics and econometrics can profitably be used in several

fields of history, including some of the oldest and most intensively culti-
vated ones. To this extent at least the proud title of 'new economic
history' has justified itself, for as long as its claim to novelty is based on
the novelty of its techniques, nobody will dispute it.

But it would be disputed if it were claimed not only for the methods of
new economic history, but also for its contents. Critics might then refuse
the claim to novelty to historical studies whose frontiers and choice of
themes have remained unaltered. As far as its themes go, the main effects
of the new economic history have been to correct the accepted versions of
familiar historical events rather than to raise new problems or to contribute to the elucidation of economic propositions. If so, the critics particular
about titles might be justified in regarding the new economic history as but
the old economic history writ mathematical.

VI

The worth of theoretical infections is not, of course, that of mere novelty,
but that of renovation – renovation by continuous expansion of interests.
It is perhaps too early to decide whether the expansion has invariably
conferred any 'feedback' benefits on the social sciences themselves.
Historians' intended contributions to theory still bear an unwelcome
family resemblance to the lessons of history of a century ago. What
redeems them is the hope that greater profit could come from history
employed in conjunction with a theoretical argument, and as one of its
stages, than from the lessons of history old-style offered as substitutes
for theory.

Even to the historian the inter-commoning with social sciences may be
fraught with difficulties. The difficulties are partly human. The ability
to profit from proximity to social sciences requires tastes and aptitudes
which many historians do not claim and do not even wish to possess.
Professional historians are apt to be drawn to their profession by an
aversion from theory and its procedures. Such historians, even when they
wish to stay attuned to the world, may find it easier to get its sounds by
ear than to receive them transmitted and transformed by philosophy and
the social sciences.

Yet even if on personal grounds the pursuit of theory-oriented history
were easier than some historians find it, it would still possess what most
of them would regard as a crippling drawback – that of sectoral specialization. Theory-oriented history justifies, indeed necessitates, the separate
existence of specialized branches, and must perpetuate the sub-division

of historical study by 'aspects'. An historian sharing his problems with social scientists must be sufficiently intimate with the latters' problems to spot in them the proper points of entry for himself. He must be able to formulate his questions and to shape his answers in a manner particular to the social science he happens to communicate with, and to use, or at least to understand, its language. So conducted, historical studies may be difficult to fit with other branches of history similarly specialized and even more difficult to combine with straightforward narrative histories unconcerned with any theoretical problems of politics, economy or society.

However, set against the actual performance of historians, as distinct from their professional ambition, this particular price is not very exorbitant. Had the universal and general story of the past been within historians' reach, anything making it more difficult for any historians to share in it might deserve to be condemned as a costly diversion. In these circumstances even economic historians might think twice before casting their studies into a shape that would not fit into an integrated history of mankind. But, with the prospects of current intellectual activities being what they are, the loss of place in general history could be well outpriced by the gain of sharing in the buildup of a social science, be it even the dismal science of economics.

What may make the price all the easier to bear is that at its very highest it need not compel the historian to sacrifice the most permanent, the truly entailed, part of his intellectual patrimony. The attitudes which historians and philosophers of history have always regarded as the hallmarks of historical study need not, indeed cannot, be discarded. No matter how inextricable his involvement with the social sciences or how high his hopes for the general laws of social theory, the historian must, as long as his work is historical, cast his studies in the concrete and in the unique.

Historical study must be presented in the concrete. I have argued that the historian's facts, i.e. the aspects of events he observes and studies, are abstracted from the infinite indefinite totality of past experience. But the abstraction of his observable facts does not free the historian from the compulsion to build up his subject as fully as he can and to assemble its detailed features into a consistent shape or physiognomy. The historical study must preserve its appearance of a portrait: a recognizable likeness of an actual man or of an identifiable group of men, or of a real occurrence.

It matters not that in the hands of scientists historical portraits may lose some of their virtue as likenesses. Scientists may try to assemble historical portraits into collections, and so to light and arrange them as to bring out some of their features to the disregard of others. Such employment of historical studies need not, however, affect the procedures of the historical student himself. Whatever the final uses to which his studies may be put, their immediate product must be firmly situated in its time, place and accidental environment and be fully built up from its detailed characteristics. In short, it must appear concrete.

It must also appear to be unique. A phenomenon as it presents itself to an historian and is presented by him, is an individual occurrence. Its uniqueness is, of course, a counterpart of its concreteness. The particular position of an event in time and place will not combine with the particular assortment of its characteristics and will not fit into its accidental environment, except once and once only. To this extent history is made up not only of portraits but of biographies – stories of lives, combinations of individual lives or happenings, all seemingly individual and unrepeatable.

Such stories, however individual, can be combined in a series and manipulated to exhibit some of their common incidents; and the latter could be used by social scientists to support generalized propositions. But however promising these generalized uses of individual stories can be, it should not divert the historian from the historical ways. In order to remain an historian and to preserve the historical character of his contribution to social science the historian must proceed as if his subjects were all individual and unique.

'As if' is the operative term. A problem-oriented history must be dressed up as individual and concrete; but the dress will often disguise the real anatomy and functions of the underlying body of facts. A study whose topics are the problems of social sciences or practical concerns of politics, whose facts are relevant aspects of events, whose ambition is to contribute to the proof or refutation of theoretical propositions, must always try and reach out of the individual and the concrete to the general and the universal.

Yet even if the concrete and unique appearance of the historian's facts may be somewhat fictitious – a mere garb – he must not dress them otherwise. His evidence and his tools of analysis and, above all, his means of expression will leave him no choice. Above all, he will not be able to satisfy his or his readers' hankering after generalizations cast in universal terms.

The facts of history, its very evidence, are too complex to yield simple generalizations. To put it into more mathematical terms, the facts of history cannot be cast into equations yielding single solutions. However fully an historical fact has been detached from the underlying event, and however close-fitting its relevance is to a social problem, its detachment can never be so full and its relevance as precise as they can be in physical objects 'isolated' for scientific experiment. A social equation will of necessity be multi-variable, and its solution will be not in the nature of a single answer or one firm expectation, but in that of a range of alternative possibilities and forecasts. And a range of multiple solutions cannot be presented as a generalized law or a categorical prediction of science.

The language of history will also make it difficult for the historian to present his results in a generalized and universalized form. Historians must employ a vocabulary charged with all the variable meanings of which words are capable. Even if mathematical formulae could be used in presenting historical conclusions they would not rid historical propositions of their imprecision and instability. For as long as the symbols of mathematics are truly symbolical, they would represent social concepts first conceived in words, and would merely carry over into mathematical formulae the ambiguity of their verbal prototypes. The products of historical inquiry must therefore remain not only complex and uncertain in substance, but also imprecise and unstable in expression.

The double curse – that of facts which are too complex for simple equations, and of words too uncertain for unambiguous formulation – is not confined to historical study. It afflicts all social sciences, though some of them (social anthropology in the first instance) may have learned how to live with it. But whether because they are specially concerned with facts, or whether because their facts are specially resistant to generalizations or whether because their study has suffered most from premature and faulty lessons, historians are, and should be, better aware of their inability to propound general laws and to use universal terms than other social scientists.

Their preference must be for generalizations which are not formulated but merely implied. They would imply the existence of underlying social laws by showing how a seemingly concrete phenomenon is shaped by the actions of general forces; they could make a unique phenomenon reflect the laws of society by presenting it as a microcosm – a particle of a universe and of a flow of events much wider than itself.

In his own tongue-tied way the most orthodox of historians will sometimes show himself to be aware of the generalizations implicit in seemingly unique and concrete works of history, and may even betray his appreciation of them. He will as a rule express his appreciation in the everyday language of non-philosophical scholarship; and the word he would probably use would be 'suggestive'. He might, of course, be surprised to be told that what the word expresses is the recognition and commendation of the generalized and abstract implications of an historical study. But what else can it connote than the idea – may it be a mere suspicion – that the study in question has a bearing on historical situations other than those it directly deals with, or that its conclusions shed light on a range of issues transcending that of its ostensible subject?

The problem-oriented historian need not restrict himself to words as homely as this; nor need he be unaware of the scientific generalization implied in his study. Yet he, no more than the fact-bound scholar, cannot exhibit his generalizations except by implication, or pursue them except by trying to catch the reflection of the general or the universal in the unique and the concrete.

To an historian these oblique ways (to an unfriendly critic they might appear hidden as well as oblique) are no more than a *pis aller*: the best he could do with his facts. They are bound to be imperfect: and their most crippling imperfection is the requirements they impose not only on the historian but also on his public. To present reflected and implied general-izations as part of a meaningful science of society is to assume a relation between a real historian and his public parallel to that between a true poet and his readers. A truly poetic message will be found contained within a whole range of meanings capable of being read into a poetic utterance. It must be so contained because, being poetic, it is bound to be too subtle, too complex, and too elusive to be unambiguously conveyed by a simple humdrum word. The historic utterance, like the poetic one, also assumes a public sensitive to its 'suggestions', i.e. sufficiently perceptive to be able to recognize the general and abstract implications of individual and concrete stories, and sometimes even to discern the particular degree and version of generality which a science-oriented historian has tried to impart to his subject.

In short, problem-oriented history is a difficult enterprise, difficult for all concerned. Its facts are intellectual constructs, even if rooted in reality; its objectives are scientific laws which cannot be expressed as such; its practitioners must combine the striving for the general with the concentration on the concrete and the individual; its readers require the same depth and subtlety of understanding which goes into the writing of scientific history at its best. But the difficulty is inherent in the very enterprise of social science. The only way to avoid it is to study history without trying to understand it: which is what some historians and so many of their readers in fact do. The moment the historian conceives the ambition to understand, and conducts his historical studies accordingly, he brings upon himself the curse of *homo sapiens*. After all, Adam's curse was to labour not with the grease of his elbow but with the sweat of his brow.

6

ECONOMIC AND SOCIAL HISTORY[1]

The study of economic history is now a flourishing pursuit; flourishing even by the standards of our inflationary age. There are new chairs and readerships in almost every British university, lectureships and research studentships galore, a busy Economic History Society, a *Review* with a circulation larger than that of any other comparable historical journal here or abroad, and several specialized journals devoted to the history of transport, agriculture, technology. Above all, a stream of articles and books, both recondite and popular, has been flowing in great and rising volume.

The prosperity is due to many causes, some of which are obviously adventitious. If so much is now being done in the field of business history, and we are promised a whole library of books on the pattern of Mr Wilson's successful history of Unilever's, this is obviously due not only to the attractions of 'entrepreneurial' problems, but also to the blandishments of a number of old and wealthy firms. Similarly, if the recent history of the engineering industry, of the armament industry, of shipping, of the distributive trades and – most important of all – of national incomes and outlays, has been subjected to detailed study, the credit for this belongs to official and corporate sponsors of every kind, and above all, to Her Majesty's Government and the National Institute of Social and Economic Research.

Among the extraneous advantages which the subject now enjoys, one must also reckon the support which it has been receiving from its fellow-travellers. Thus, local antiquarians, though as a rule uncommitted to economic history as it is understood nowadays, have been nevertheless providing economic historians both with raw material and with semi-manufactured components. Equally unsolicited, and equally unearned, has been the support which the study of economic history has always received from Marxists, and more especially from the younger Marxists,

---

[1] First published in *The Times Literary Supplement*, 6 January 1956.

65

who flock to the subject in the vain hope of finding in it an economic interpretation of history.

Nevertheless this outside bounty alone will not account for the recent expansion of the subject. The main drive has come from within, from a doctrinal pressure which has been gathering for a number of years, even if it did not break out into the open till very recently. This, of course, is not the first time that the students of economic history find themselves propelled by an accumulated pressure of submerged ideas. For a subject so respectable and so well received, economic history has a commendable record of intellectual inconstancy. In this country it began at the turn of the century under auspices which were largely political. Two of its founders and authors of standard treatises, Archdeacon Cunningham and Sir William Ashley, derived from the German traditions of the historical school of political economy and the *Kathedersozialisten*. Like their German prototypes, they were primarily interested in the economic policies of the State and sought to establish an intellectual arsenal for the imperialist and protectionist campaigns of New Toryism. Their medievalist contemporaries were, of course, unconcerned with Joseph Chamberlain's ideals, but their inspiration was also very largely German, legal-political, and as such, highly anachronistic. Their preoccupation with the personal status of medieval villeins reflected, fifty or seventy years after the event and hundreds of miles away from the original scene, the battles for the emancipation of the serfs in Germany and Russia.

The next generation, that of Unwin, the Webbs, Cole and Tawney, moved away both from the German precept and from the Tory inspiration. The political interest, however, remained, even if the emphasis shifted leftward, from tariff reform to socialist reconstruction. Tawney, the greatest and still the most influential of them, is, of course, too rich and too many-sided a mind to follow a single track; and his work not only reflects the historical and political interests of his generation, but also presages some of the historical issues under discussion at the present time. Yet no reader of his books can fail to notice the thread which binds together his famous tract on *The Acquisitive Society*, his introduction to Wilson's *Usury*, his essay on *Religion and the Rise of Capitalism*, and his treatise on *The Agrarian Problem in the Sixteenth Century*. There is no denying that he owes his great influence as much to the appeal of his politics and ethics as to the power of his historical scholarship or to the bewitchment of his Miltonic prose.

Whether to its credit or its disgrace, the present, the third, generation of economic historians finds itself less directly inspired by political ideas (some indirect inspiration there is bound to be), and is more purely academic and theoretical, in the good and bad senses of the terms. Its main stimuli come from within the university, and more especially from some of the academic fields on which it borders. The involvement of economic historians with the theoretical problems of economics is, of course, older than our post-war world. A proportion of economic historians have always regarded themselves as economists by free choice; many of them teach in the faculties of economics, and are, to that extent, economists by compulsion. Their students and their readers often expect them to discuss in relation to the past the same problems which economic theoreticians discuss in relation to our own times, or in the timeless vacuum they have made their own. There is thus nothing surprising in the interest which the economic historians of the 1930s took in the history of crises and commercial fluctuations: an interest which, owing to the time-lag inherent in historical research, still exerts its belated influence on the work of some economic historians of our own day.

However, it is only since the war that economic historians have found themselves exposed to the full blast of economic debate. What has happened is that economists have moved *en masse* to the very frontiers of economic history and brought their climate with them. Having exhausted the intellectual and practical possibilities of their inherited technique – that of abstract analysis of 'short-term' or 'static' problems – and having in addition been called upon to advise governments on the economic development of backward countries, the economists now find themselves drawn more and more into the discussion of economic growth through generations and centuries. Some of them try to tackle the problem in the way most congenial to them, that of the mathematical 'models'. Most economists, however, realize that by changing over from 'short' to 'long', from the problems of, say, commercial crises to those of economic progress, they have entered the world of history. And what drags them into that world is not only the extended time-scale of their problem but also its subject-matter – technology, population, value-judgments, &c. – to which the techniques of economics are ill adapted, but which form the stock-in-trade of economic history.

Needless to say, the historical and sociological inquiries called forth by the new interest in growth will sometimes be made by economists themselves (*vide* Professor Lewis's latest book) and enjoy all the advantages and disadvantages of amateur endeavour. But on the whole the economists will expect historians to do the job and to join them in the discussion of economic development – presumably in the manner in which this was done at the recent conference on economic growth in Santa Marguerita. This is an invitation historians cannot refuse and which they have shown every sign of accepting. Some, like Walt Rostow, have responded not only by affirming the historical character of the problem but also by offering a complete blue-print for its solution. Others have busied themselves with redoubled energy and a sense of mission in the study of population, capital accumulation, industrialization, motivation of labour, behaviour patterns of entrepreneurs, incentives of saving, and other 'constituent topics' of economic growth. Others still, more especially the medievalists, have turned to the study of 'trends', or the alternative phases in the economic ascent of western Europe. It is round topics like these that most of the current researches now cluster. It is also on these topics that the critics of British economic historiography, mostly Russian and Polish, have trained their fire; and it was these topics that filled most of the sessions devoted to economic history at the recent International Historical Congress in Rome.

Thus propelled, the study of economic history is now going full-steam ahead. But, even if sailing at full speed promises to shorten the journey, it will add little to its comforts. The discomforts of this particular journey have not as yet shown themselves in full. But if and when they do they will inevitably reveal the unsettled and uneasy relations between the members of the crew. In the past, economic historians engaged on joint tasks with the economists were sometimes expected to work to the latter's orders – i.e. to take their formulation of problems, their terms and their concepts and apply them to historical material. Even in the past historians frequently found the tools of the economists difficult to manipulate; in future such manipulations may prove well-nigh impossible. As I have already observed, the regions in which the answers to the problem of growth lie hidden are well outside the economists' home country. They are all buried in the 'social framework' of economics and are resistant to treatment by the conventional methods of economists. If so, it is difficult to see how and in what form economists, *qua* economists, can contribute to the historical study of economic growth. A clear and consistent system of terms and concepts will be indispensable, but will it come on loan from the economists, as hitherto, or will it have to be improvised by historians themselves?

It is perhaps too much to hope that the theoretical aid will come from sociologists. The lack of sociological inspiration in the study and writing of economic history is a frequently voiced complaint. However narrowly economic may be the preoccupations of some economic historians, their material and their processes of thought are of necessity sociological. In this context, however, the word 'sociological' denotes not a system of thought permeating all social studies, but a hungry void, a sinking feeling, in their midst. Much as some economic historians would have wished to possess themselves of a sociological framework into which to fit their historical facts, no such framework has yet been devised. Some American historians have imported Talcot Parsons's notion of 'social role' into their study of entrepreneurial behaviour, but this single importation has not grown into a real intellectual commerce, and there is apparently very little chance of it doing so.

These are, in short, the discomforts of travelling fast towards a well-defined and alluring destination, and yet without much help from the members of the crew who would normally be expected to steer the course. And the discomforts of the journey are not made any lighter by the growing distance from the *terra firma* of conventional narrative history. True enough, the position of the economic historian on this *terra* has never been very easy. In general, ordinary historians have little sympathy for the real business of economic history and lose interest in the work of economic historians as soon as it departs from the familiar milestones of past politics. And, unfortunately, depart it must. In their attempts to understand and to display the process of economic and social change economic historians have acquired a point of view and an assortment of topics which do not fit into the conventional narrative, whether political or diplomatic or constitutional. Their landmarks, their terms, indeed their very centuriation of history are different.

The main difference, however, is in the choice of problems. Nowadays economic historians choose them not from among the familiar events and personalities of history, but from the hypotheses of social sciences. The relation between aggregate output of agriculture and the productivity of new land, the 'terms of trade' between agriculture and industry, the effects of supply of bullion and of population trends on the movements of prices, the part which technical change played in the evolution of industry – these are a fair sample of the topics which now occupy the medieval economic historians. What agitates the modernists are problems like relative contributions of birth rates and death rates to long-term trends of population, the validity of the Marxian hypothesis of expropriation of peasant landholders as a pre-requisite of the Industrial Revolution, the influence of the rate of interest on the supply of capital, the behaviour of business men in different phases of industrial development, the responsiveness of labour to the economic stimuli of wages.

Is it, then, surprising that historians should sometimes find it hard to absorb the output of economic history? Some historians are catholic enough to add bits of 'economic' matter or 'social' atmosphere to their mainly political writings. Others go as far as to impute 'economic causes' to the wars and the revolutions in which they happen to be interested. The most catholic among the leading historians, like the Provost of Oriel or the Master of Peterhouse, may try and assemble their 'general' history out of the specialized histories of science, religion, or economics, introducing them in the order in which they happen to have been picked out by the limelight of historical tradition: art in the fifteenth century, religion in the sixteenth, science in the seventeenth, economics in the eighteenth.

This, of course, is better than nothing, but even at its best this does not solve the problem of the proper relations of economic and general history. Nor has the solution been advanced, if anything it has been impeded, by some of the intellectual fashions in the teaching and writing of history. The plea for general 'undifferentiated' history has often gone together with the spirit of anti-intellectual holism. The argument is usually compounded of truths and half-truths dear to the hearts of historians – the indivisible unity of historical process, the unpredictability of historical events, the unrepeatable individuality of historical phenomena, the virtue of feeling and imagination as means of historical understanding, the inadequacy of positive thought and scientific analysis. In an atmosphere so charged the least rationalist of economic historians might stand out as an alien. As for economic historians post-war vintage, involved as they are in the problems of growth and mixing as they do with economists and sociologists (and of late, even with geographers and ecologists), they might well appear and be treated as the fifth column.

Fortunately the holist mood now shows signs of dissolving. Equally fortunately some of the other current fashions are less concerned with fundamentals of historical method and come very near to the business if not to the spirit of economic and social history. One is the interest which political and constitutional historians of the sixteenth and the eighteenth centuries have of late shown in what they term social history. It matters little that much of it appears to lack intellectual purpose; that it merely leaves out the 'logical' from the 'sociological'; and that it sometimes differs from old-fashioned political history merely in its preference for biographies of unimportant people or for the humdrum moments in the lives of famous men. Provided the chosen people are really unimportant and the chosen moments really humdrum, the social historians of this type will without wishing it supply the grist for the mills of sociology and economic history. And in the meantime the essays, even if their inspiration be 'all garter and no merit', will be read and probably enjoyed by the general.

Yet another bridge has of late been thrown over the gap by the economic historians themselves. Students of agrarian history have lately been turning to the history of the land itself. This new activity, at its higher flights, is very much involved with economic growth. But its lower ranges, the researches it has promoted and the writings it has produced, offer numerous attractions both to practitioners and to the readers of general history. Its themes – the individual villages, farms and fields of rustic England – are concrete and familiar, and conjure up visual images without suppressing intellectual, or if you wish, scientific purposes. In this respect the history of agriculture, with its evocation of landscape and the open air, has perhaps an unfair advantage over other topics of economic history. But the points from which the ordinary historian or reader of history books can see and appreciate the work of economic historians are so few that we must be doubly grateful for this particular belvedere.

7

ECONOMIC GROWTH[1]

No economic historian, however insulated from contact with economic or any other theory, can fail to notice the recent invasions of his territory by economic theorists and statisticians. Before the war theoretical economists were not, on the whole, much active in his immediate neighbourhood. Their main interests at that time centred on the trade cycle and on the related problems of the short-term equilibrium, and these could be, and in fact were, discussed against a supposedly unchanging historical background. Since the war, however, economic discussion has largely shifted to long-term problems, to secular trends, to factors of growth and decline: all of them topics very near the historian's home.

The new interest in evolutionary topics partly reflects the practical occupations of post-war economists. In the last few years they have been called upon to pronounce on at least two related issues which cannot be discussed on the assumption that time stands still. One is that of the 'speed up' of the industrialized economics in Western Europe, and the other is that of the 'build up' of the backward economics of Africa and East Asia. Both issues are concerned with growth and decline over long periods of continuous development and are to that extent 'historical'.

Practical necessity is not, however, alone to blame or to thank for the new orientation. To borrow an adjective much favoured by economists, the invention of the 'long-term' theories has to some extent been 'autonomous', i.e. a further stage in the expansion of a developing doctrine. For years before the war economists tried to break out of the bounds of 'static' and 'particular', i.e. one-commodity, equilibria within which the 'marginal' theories then largely dwelled. Attempts to construct theoretical models applicable to problems of general equilibrium, i.e. to the functioning of entire economic systems, occupied a number of younger economists in the thirties; and for the same reasons, attempts to construct so-called 'dynamic' models, i.e. theoretical devices for dealing

---

[1] A review of W. W. Rostow, *The Process of Economic Growth* (Oxford: Clarendon Press, 1953), first published in *The Economic History Review*, Second Series, vol. VI, no. 1, 1953.

with economic change over long periods of time, were also bound to come.

In this way, under a double inspiration, economists have now moved into regions which historians have always regarded as their own. Yet, so far, the growing proximity has not done much to bring historical and theoretical study together. Perhaps nearest to history in form and substance has been the work of statisticians and econometricians, for some of the statistical series they have produced in recent years reach into the very heart of the economic history of the nineteenth century. On the other hand, in the so-called 'dynamic' theories, especially those conceived in this country, economic growth figures as an assumption hypothetical in form and non-historical in content. All they can do is to disclose the manner in which change over long periods might affect the mechanism of economic adjustments hitherto studied in its short-term setting; and more especially the relations between income, saving, investment and employment. In other words, to economists 'growth' is not so much a problem for analysis, as a new set of conditions in which their old problems are set. In so far as they have explored the process of growth instead of merely assuming it, they have been apt to confine themselves to the theory of capital formation which has always figured as, so to speak, a 'long-term' element within the short-term theory.[1]

On their part economic historians have been singularly insensitive to theoretical movements on their flanks. In Britain they may sometimes have made use of Colin Clark's statistical speculations, as an aid to teaching. In the United States, Schumpeter's well-known book, with its emphasis on the formative role of the entrepreneur, has stimulated and sustained the work of 'entrepreneurial' histories. But these two treatises apart (and both lie away from the mainstream of modern theoretical debate), none of the recent writing and discussion of 'dynamic' economics, or of theories of growth, has had much effect on the study of economic history by historians. The range of economic subjects studied by them still appears to be

[1] Of the recent British theorists who have published books on the subject, R. F. Harrod is preoccupied with the relation of income to saving consistent with continued advance of income, given the social framework, increasing population and technological progress (*Towards a Dynamic Economics*, 1948). Mrs Joan Robinson (*The Rate of Interest and Other Essays*, 1951) is mainly concerned with employment in a developing economy. She takes account of the various determinants of output over long periods of time (the 'vicissitudes' of a developing economy) but does not make them the subject of her inquiry. The growth of capital is perhaps the only determinant which she does not take for granted but subjects to causal analysis. Professor Hicks is also mainly concerned with the adjustment of his theoretical system, essentially 'short term', to the assumption of a long-term expansion of saving and investment (*Value and Capital*, 1938 and *The Trade Cycle*, 1950).

largely unrelated to any economic theory, old or new. And it is perhaps characteristic of the historians' lack of interest in theoretical fashions that the economic problem to occupy post-war historians most, should have been that of economic fluctuations, mostly short-term fluctuations, in the seventeenth, eighteenth and nineteenth centuries.

II

From this point of view Professor Rostow's book is a new departure and a very important event in the literature of economic history. In it, for the first time, the future of dynamic economics is surveyed from the point of view of the historian, and a share in the enterprise is staked out on his behalf. Both the survey and the claim are obviously the products of wide reading, of concentrated and highly independent thought, and of an intimate understanding of attitudes and procedures of both economists and historians. No other economist, and certainly no other historian, moves in the borderland between economics and history with the same ease as Professor Rostow, and nobody else but he could have tackled the subject of his present book with greater skill and authority. It is therefore a safe prophecy that much of his argument will command universal assent among economic historians and will sooner or later form part of their orthodox tradition.

In brief, Professor Rostow's argument is that a theory of economic growth can emerge only from a study of those social factors which were in the past and must remain in the future the material of economic history – changes in technology, in tastes and in quantities of resources. But if historical study of this material is to make its contribution to a theory of growth it must be fitted into a theoretical enterprise *ab initio*, i.e. must be so limited and so directed as to be able to answer questions which a theory of economic growth will pose. Having thus made the case for a historical study serving theoretical purposes, Professor Rostow proceeds to enumerate and to define the theoretical objects thus to be served. In addition, the concluding three chapters of the book reproduce some of Professor Rostow's historical studies, presumably on the assumption that they provide examples of historical studies harnessed to dynamic theory.

The argument is thus both general and particular, and provides a prospectus of the theory of growth as a whole, as well as a detailed inventory of its contents. But on the whole, it is in Professor Rostow's general argument, rather than in the detailed layout of dynamic theory, that his most authoritative and convincing ideas will be found.

Economic growth

Most convincing of all is, of course, his demonstration that the study of economic development is not the kind of enterprise that economic theorists can further without the massive aid of the historian and of the sociologist. Some historians may even be prepared to go further and argue that the study of growth calls for equipment and techniques antithetic to all the ingrained habits of economic thought. To study the problems of long-term development is to invert the logical order of economic propositions and to transpose the things which theoreticians consider as problems and things which they take as 'given'. In conventional economic analysis factors like technical progress, changes in tastes, or movements in population, are, for the purposes of argument, assumed as constant. This assumption is perfectly legitimate within the limits of short-term problems. Readjustments of a short-term equilibrium are, by definition, instantaneous or all but instantaneous; and while they take place, technology, tastes, population and the other 'external' factors must remain to all intents and purposes unchanged. But the assumption of unchanged external factors becomes more fictitious and false as the time-scale is extended, until it becomes wholly untenable in the 'secular' periods in which the problems of economic growth have to be set. Within these periods the significant movements are those which take place among the facts of social life which the economists have been in the habit of regarding as constant. Compared to them the short-term changes in supply and demand are unimportant and often irrelevant: Clapham's 'ripples on the broad heave of historical change'.

Thus, in changing over from 'short' to 'long', the economists must not only alter their time-scale, but also transfer their studies from the conventional subjects of economics to those which have hitherto formed the stock-in-trade of economic historians. This some individual economists will doubtless be able to do without much trouble or pain. Some have done this already and are doing it every time they are called upon to discuss Britain's or the world's distant prospects. Economic journalists nowadays manipulate trends, real and imaginary, past and present, as to the manner born, and some of them have been doing this since the earliest days of economic journalism; indeed more so in the days of Bagehot than now. In his days, and before him, the main body of economic doctrine was compounded of notions which were largely 'dynamic' and was accordingly shot through with what would now be considered as history or sociology. Ricardo's theory of investment and rent, his and Rodbertus's theory of wages, the Malthusian theory of population, were nothing if not 'long-term', and were, through Marx, able to inspire the only complete theory

75

of economic development so far propounded. Occasional particles of history and more than occasional particles of sociology will be found even in John Stuart Mill; and Alfred Marshall ranged freely over the past and the future, especially in his *Industry and Trade*, and knowingly speculated about economic growth in terms patently historical.

Yet for all this intermingling of the 'static' and the 'dynamic', of economics and history, the fact remains that it is not at the points of intermingling that the characteristic contributions of economic theory will be found. The advancement of economic doctrine, especially since the days of Menger and Jevons and within the world of ideas which since their day economists have inhabited, has been dependent on attitudes of mind and on a method of investigation as clearly differentiated from that of historians or anthropologists as any intellectual process can be. And it is this differentiation that, on Professor Rostow's showing, will have to be broken down in the process of constructing a theory of economic growth. That theory will have to advance along the same road and by the same vehicles as those now used for their travels by historians.

III

To accept Professor Rostow's argument is to pass upon the shoulders of historians the main responsibility for the theory of economic growth. But this responsibility cannot be discharged without some reorientation of historical studies. It will require from historians a certain minimum of relevance; in this particular case of relevance to the main problems of economic development.

It can, of course, be argued that most historical work is, indeed cannot help being, relevant to economic development. Professor Rostow himself, writing in a mood of universal tolerance and optimism, tries to demonstrate how much economic history so far written has already contributed to our understanding of economic growth. But Professor Rostow does not of course believe that the main contributions of history should be confined to accidental by-products of researches ostensibly devoted to other objects. He obviously wants historians to assume clearly defined tasks capable of filling known gaps in the main structure of theory. The historian must thus be not only sufficiently ambitious to pursue theoretical objectives, but also sufficiently modest to confine his energies to objectives allotted to him in the common enterprise.

Neither the ambition nor the modesty will be alien to the temper in which economic historians nowadays pursue their studies and will not repel anybody other than the few who have been drawn into the field of economic history by its antiquarian attractions. Nevertheless, even the historians who accept in principle the composite and co-operative nature of Professor Rostow's enterprise may find it difficult to harness themselves to the topics he has prefabricated for them.

The topics will be found in the middle chapters of his book in which he breaks down the problem of economic growth into subdivisions, each corresponding to a social tendency whose pace and direction can be expected to influence economic development. There is thus the tendency to consume and to save, the tendency to engage in pure and applied science, the tendency to breed children. Each of these is in its turn revealed as a composite of other social trends, and the presumption is that all these tendencies and subtendencies must serve as the historian's points of relevance, the hooks on which he will hang the products of his inquiries. And although Professor Rostow is careful not to assume that historians will receive their detailed hypotheses out of a general dispensary, instead of conceiving them in the course of their researches, the very nature of his 'propensities' and the purposes for which they appear to have been devised, may raise in the minds of a reader a number of awkward questions.

Above all, historians will have every reason to feel puzzled by Professor Rostow's confidence that the problem of economic growth, so broken down, could in the end be reassembled into a fully articulated theory. If he expects historical inquiries to make their contributions to certain precise and predetermined points in the theory of economic growth he must obviously expect them to yield results radically different from the habitual products of historical inquiry. Will they be in the form of general propositions expressed in universal terms and capable of mathematical or quasi-mathematical manipulation by economic analysts? If, on the other hand, he does not expect historical inquiries to abandon the empirical and concrete study of individual situations, by what magic and by what magicians will its results be transmuted into parts of an abstract and a universal theory of economic growth?

As Professor Rostow is himself an outstanding historian, we must assume that he does not expect any such transmutation to take place. But in that case the difference between economics of the 'short-term' or 'static' kind and the economic theory of growth is even more profound than Professor Rostow's general chapters make it to be. For in that case the shift from 'short' to 'long' will signify not only a transposition of what is asked and what is given but also a fundamental difference in the logical nature of the results. Indeed the difference is bound to be fully as wide as that which now distinguishes truths discoverable by historical investigation from those demonstrable in economic theory.

The difference is inherent in the two respective subject matters. The factors 'external' to economic analysis which are now the preserve of the economic historian are his not merely because the economist has been content to leave them alone. They have been eschewed by economists because they cannot be fully accounted for as mere quantities dependent on changing volumes of income and because for this and other reasons they do not lend themselves to the so-called deductive manipulation characteristic of economic theory or of formal logic.[1] And they have been adopted by historians because they can be understood only as facets of an integrated social process, or as interrelated parts of a single 'organism'. The trivial and utterly irrelevant conclusions which Kelsen derived from his deductive study of political actions of the *homo politicus* have fortunately put an end to all endeavours to introduce into the study of politics the dialectical abstractions of Viennese economics. More recently an ingenious, if somewhat humourless, attempt to construct a mathematical model of committee government has demonstrated to the great satisfaction of the Philistines, the dangers of importing the methods of modern econometrics into the study of the machinery of government. Similarly, technological progress, development of science, changes in human tastes and motives, indeed most of Professor Rostow's 'propensities' and factors behind them, will defy all attempts at being analysed in the manner of Menger or Walras.[2]

If so, can we ever expect the study of economic growth to achieve the worth and dignity of what many of Rostow's readers, if not Professor Rostow himself, commonly understand by the term theory? That a state of greater wisdom may result from the concrete, empirical and individualized researches of historians and sociologists goes without saying. Historical description, be it never so earthbound or rooted in the past, may enable us to discriminate between the typical and generic features of certain situations, and may in the end narrow down the range of our expectations. But how can the indeterminate and even inchoate intel-

---

[1] In Professor Rostow's words, the 'propensities' are 'determined by a complex of forces largely independent...of short-term changes of income...Only in a roundabout, long-run manner are the propensities linked to the level of income.' *Op. cit.* p. 37.
[2] Apparently it was considerations of this character that led Alfred Marshall to take a frankly agnostic view of the prospects of a theory of long-term equilibria. *Principles of Economics*, Appendix H; *Money, Credit and Commerce*, Appendix J; Rostow, *op. cit.* p. 6, and also p. 37.

lectual products of inquiries like these be allotted shares in a single theoretical undertaking?

Historians can further the study of economic growth (indeed they cannot help doing so), but it is doubtful whether they will do their furthering in a manner different from that in which history in general has so far been serving the philosophy of life and society, i.e. by that process of indirect and reflected enlightenment which can sometimes illuminate the hidden recesses of reality, but which will defy all attempts to fix it in a mathematical, or even a verbal, formula, and still more to turn it into heat capable of raising steam for a useful piece of political or economic machinery.

Of these limitations Professor Rostow himself is of course well aware. In his own words 'a theoretical formulation can pretend to no more... than a more coherent and unified treatment of particular situations' (p. 8). Elsewhere (pp. 45–50) he also tries to allow full weight to the objection against the 'formulation by those concerned with one discipline of questions to be answered by those working in other disciplines'. Only as long as Professor Rostow is able to sustain this sober and reticent mood will historians be able to accept his hopeful definition of their theoretical mission.

8

A PLAGUE OF ECONOMISTS?

ON SOME CURRENT MYTHS, ERRORS,
AND FALLACIES[1]

I

Inquisitions by economists and economic journalists into Britain's predicament are in no danger of running out of indictable culprits. The Trade Unions, the working class as a whole, the Chancellor of the Exchequer, the Bank of England, the international monetary authorities, and, of course, Harold Wilson, each of them separately and all of them in combination have been named as the guilty ones. At no time, however, has any guilt been imputed to the inquisitors themselves, the economists of England. Yet on any impartial allocation of blame a share must attach to the economic experts.

It is not that the quality of British economics, or economists, has sunk and now stands lower than in the past or than in other, less afflicted, countries. On the contrary, judged by the numbers of its professional practitioners and its lay addicts, economics was never more flourishing. The voice of academic economists was never louder and was never heard with greater awe. Nor is there much wrong about the quality of the economists themselves. In recent years Cambridge may have yielded the leadership in pure theory to MIT, Stanford, or Chicago, but the University which still boasts of Joan Robinson, Nicholas Kaldor, J. R. N. Stone, Piero Sraffa, and a multitude of gifted youngsters, has every right to be as immodest about its intellectual standing as it apparently is. The same is to a large extent true of the reconstructed Department of Economics at LSE or of Oxford or Colchester. It is also true of the intellectual quality of the economists in government service. The economists at the Department of Economic Affairs are led by a man of the highest intelligence and experience, who is well matched by several economists in the same and other departments. Above all, there is Professor Kaldor, whose qualities of near-genius – originality, mental vigour, and a capacity for inspired hunches – will be admitted by his worst enemies. In short,

[1] First published in *Encounter*, January 1968.

judged by professional standards, the quality of British economics still ranks very high and is not in question.

What is more questionable are the standards themselves, or to be more exact, the professional qualifications and attitudes which the economists bring, and are expected to bring, to their governmental and journalistic jobs. Are the contents of modern economics, the ideas with which the economists operate as relevant to the economic problems of our age as they and their public believe? Have they with their models, measurements and forecasts, helped the economic recovery, or have they, on the contrary, aggravated Britain's predicament by misdirecting the attention of the government and the public?

I am afraid my answer to these questions must go against the economists. It may well be that the very quality of post-war economics, the greater sophistication of its theoretical constructions, its much refined statistical and econometric methods, have put it out of touch with real economic situations. If modern economics is frequently irrelevant to Britain's economic problem, the failure has been largely due to some of its most recent achievements – to certain conceptual features of the Keynesian theory and to the statistical classifications of economic activities and factors.

In this context it is the methodological frame of the Keynesian doctrine, not its main design, that is in question. Nobody now can or will doubt the significance of the theoretical revolution brought about by John Maynard Keynes, or disparage the immensity of its practical contribution. Of all the influences which have shaped the post-war economy, propelled the growth of national products and inspired the welfare state, full employment has obviously been the most potent; and of the influences behind the policy of full employment, the Keynesian prescriptions have been by far the most effective. The Keynesian medicine is not, however, to be had free of charge. The payment with which the man-in-the-street is most familiar and dislikes most is inflation; but the payment of which the man-in-the-street is least conscious, but which concerns us most here is the compulsive preoccupation of economists with aggregates cast on a national scale, and their neglect of the more detailed, more concrete, more (so to speak) personal and social problems of modern economy.

II

The aggregate view of the economy is Keynesian *par excellence*. Tradition will have it that the concept of aggregate demand came to him from his disciples; but having acquired it, Keynes built upon it his entire structure. And demand is not the only economic variable which Keynes treats solely in the aggregate. As the very title of his famous treatise indicates, its entire approach is generally macro-economic, as distinct from the micro-economic concern with individual enterprises and persons. The entities it operates with are all conceived as country-wide totals or as national averages. In its scheme savings, investment, labour force, the price levels, the rate of interest, are generalized holistic concepts, detached from their local and specific circumstances. Its prescriptions are therefore similarly general and holistic, or to use the biologists' jargon, 'systemic'. They are meant to be administered to the economy at its centre, so to speak by the mouth, and to be ingested and reacted to by the economic system as a whole. The principal instrument for regulating aggregate demand is fiscal measures, whether taxes or government outlays. The most powerful regulator of aggregate propensities – those to consume, to save and to invest – is the rate of interest. Employment itself is to be controlled on the same scale on which statisticians measure it, i.e. globally; and full employment is not full if it does not match all jobs with all workmen right across the economy.

It is not, therefore, surprising that in the recurrent post-war crises the Keynesian remedies advocated by economists and adopted by their Whitehall or Threadneedle Street clients should also have been mainly aggregate and holistic. All the painful dilemmas of the economy – whether to inflate or to deflate, whether to reduce comparative costs by devaluation or by universal wage freeze, whether to stimulate national investment by tax concessions or by curbs on alternative uses of savings – are posed and debated as if they affect in equal measure and in the same way all and every branch of the economy. Similarly, special surcharges on imports, higher bank rates, restrictions of credit are prescribed as general medicines, expected to work their effects through the system as a whole.

It is equally to be expected that the remedies, being systemic, should have failed to act at the points of the body economic which ailed most. Deflation did *not* stop costs and prices from rising. In 1966–7 they may have risen somewhat less steeply than in 1965, but what has held them back was not the general deflation, but the administrative and political action of the DEA and the Prices and Incomes Board. Similarly, deflation and wage freeze notwithstanding, the main drives behind the rising wage trends – the organization and policies of some Trade Unions and the ability of some industries (especially the nationalized ones) to pass on the higher costs to consumers – have remained unabated.

It is also apparent that the resources freed by deflationary curbs on consumption have not moved, as they were expected, into export industries. Exports increased slightly in 1966, but they had also been increasing in some years of comparative inflation; and it may well turn out that the most recent increases owed more to political and administrative pressures and urgings than to the spontaneous reactions of exporters to economic regulators.

As for private investment, it has not risen, but on the contrary declined, in spite of all the fiscal privileges and concealed subsidies; and the decline has been mainly due to the unpropitious psychological climate generated by deflationary measures in the industries most in need of modernization. The industries whose investment has remained buoyant are not those which government and economists would have chosen had they been able to discriminate between them, but those which happen to be relatively insulated from deflationary measures – such consumption trades as supermarkets and food industries or such nationalized industries as railways and gas.

The reason why so many of the prescriptions have failed must not be sought in their pharmacological make-up. They no doubt are the remedies appropriate to the complaints they are intended to treat. Unfortunately, the complaints they are capable of treating are *not* those which afflict British economy most painfully. The latter have as often as not been not general, not organic, but local, and not always purely economic. If the British balances of payments have been ailing, this is *not* because British exports have been relatively lower and imports relatively higher than before the war or in most other countries, but because, for reasons which are mostly political, some of the British outlays abroad are unbearably high. If the British exports have not grown sufficiently fast or consistently to eliminate all deficits in payment accounts, this is not because comparative costs and comparative prices of British export goods as a whole are higher than those of, say, German exports. They happen to be higher for some goods and not for others. The proportion of British manufactured output as a whole going into exports is higher than in any other major industrial country, with the exception of Germany. But they happen to be uncomfortably low in certain strategically situated industries, such as shipping or electrical appliances. Even where the general indices, such as rates of investment of improvement in productivity or capital-output ratios, may at first sight appear to be less favourable in the United Kingdom than in most other advanced countries, they will on further inspection turn out to be worse than abroad in some industries and firms, and better in others. And for many (perhaps most) of these local ailments the morbid causes will be found not in the malfunctioning of the life processes in the body economic, such as the low rate of savings, or the high level of prices, or the insufficient allocation of national resources to research and development, but in specific failures of its individual cells – management, design, salesmanship, or the behaviour of groups of labour.

For these morbid causes systemic medicines are an irrelevant, and sometimes even a harmful, prescription.

III

The insufficiencies, the irrelevancies, and the unforeseen side-effects of an economic advice preoccupied with the general and the overall and indifferent to the specific, local, technical and human nature of economic problems are obvious: and they are frequently acknowledged by the economists themselves. This does not, of course, mean that statesmen, officials, and business leaders can dispense altogether with it. The most common-sensical decisions on matters of practical economic detail can go awry and can have distorting effects if not considered from the point of view of the economy as a whole. Above all, the theoretical aggregates of modern economics – indices of national products, rates of growth, savings ratios, and all that – are thermometers without which the patient cannot possibly do. They measure, however crudely, the well-being of the body economic and keep it aware of its own capricious humours. What they do not and cannot do is to locate the points at which the body ails and to suggest the proper treatment for the ailment. For this a wider range of *expertise* and a wider choice of experts are needed: technicians in industry and in contact with it, industrial consultants, sociologists, and those business men who happen to know their businesses, as well as economists.

This in fact is the set-up of the French planning bodies; and even in this country this is how the 'Little Neddies' and the Prices and Incomes Board are supposed to function. In functioning bodies so set up, economists are indispensable, if only in order to save the other experts from the economic *sottises* to which non-economists are always prone. But though required to keep the other experts out of economic harm's way, economists do not hold the exclusive patent for relevant wisdom and must not claim the monopoly of advice. In matters micro-economic their role should be more cautionary than motive, though it may be more than that in matters macro-economic.

Yet, however limited in their professional role in micro-economic matters, their time and attention must be shifted bodily to them. In fact some such shift may have taken place invisibly and inaudibly. In numerous government departments, economists operate not *qua* economists, but as ordinary intelligent men, and busy themselves with the day-to-day issues of practical economic administration. We are told that of late even the topmost economists in government service (indeed Mr Kaldor himself) have gone over to concrete and detailed problems of economic and industrial policy and have shown themselves more reticent about macro-economic issues than hitherto.

IV

Unfortunately, very little of this concrete and reticent mood has reflected itself in the visible manifestations of government policy. It has been little seen in the leading articles of the financial press, and it has raised no audible echoes in the corridors of power. In these influential quarters, economic problems are still posed on the same aggregate scale and the solutions are still cast in the same generalized unspecific form as the academic solutions regularly on offer in the after-war years. Moreover, some of the economist-inspired remedies which at first sight appear wholly specific (i.e. are meant to apply only to some branches of the economy) have nevertheless turned out to be too indiscriminate and too closely related to the general theoretical concept to produce the beneficent effects expected of them.

Thus, the new corporation taxes – ostensibly a highly discriminating device – have done little to induce companies to distribute a smaller share of their profits and to increase the flow of corporate savings. Their main effect has been merely to reduce the cover for distributed profits and to make companies rely more on new issues of fixed interest stocks, than on issues of equities. The supply of equities has also been reduced and their market prices enhanced by the unforeseen effects of Capital Gains Tax. The higher taxation of companies operating abroad may have yielded higher revenue to the Exchequer, but it has not redirected resources into the domestic investment, as its authors expected it to do. Moreover (as the

Reddaway Report recognized), this particular bit of economic legislation was not sufficiently discriminate to give special treatment to firms and industries capable of employing British capital abroad with greater advantage to British economy than that to which it could be put at home.

However, the main vices of the few avowedly specific and micro-economic measures inspired by economists, come not from the aggregative and holistic preoccupations of economic theoreticians, but from the classificatory devices favoured by statisticians. Since the very early days of statistics as a social science, statisticians have adopted a 'sectoral' classification of economic activities which has now become sanctified by academic usage. They have always distinguished the so-called primary occupations, mainly agricultural, from secondary occupations, mainly manufactures. More recently, another category, that of tertiary occupations, has been constructed to accommodate the services, the liberal professions, and the various categories of national and local officialdom. On the eve of the war, this classification of economic sectors was given great publicity by Colin Clark's famous *Conditions of Economic Progress* (1940). In Clark's formulation the tripartite order of sectors was transformed from a mere classification into an itinerary of economic progress. The lesson he taught was that economic progress had been achieved in the past and was to be achieved in the future by transferring resources first from primary occupations to secondary ones and, finally, from secondary to tertiary ones.

This sectoral itinerary is now out-of-date. That its last leg – the transition from secondary to tertiary occupations – is often a symptom and a consequence of economic growth, rather than its cause, is now generally understood. Some nations have large tertiary occupations simply because they are rich enough to afford them. What is not generally understood by economists and by laymen is the optional nature of the first leg – that of growth through transfer from primary to secondary occupations.

v

Once upon a time there was an obvious justification for separating agriculture from secondary occupations and for treating it statistically and theoretically as a branch of the economy radically different from the rest. Until recently the agriculture of most European countries employed so large a share of national resources – and did so in conditions so different from those prevailing in industry – that its separate treatment offered some obvious didactic and book-writing conveniences. But, as agricultural occupations contracted and as social distinction between agricultural countryside and urban industry gradually faded, the convenience of reserving for agriculture a separate statistical and conceptual category and of treating it as an occupation radically different from other industries, has become less obvious. In these circumstances, the continued adherence to the old classification has involved economists and statesmen in an obvious 'realist' fallacy – the fallacy of assuming that the differences in words represented differences in real things.

The 'realist' fallacy has been greater still in the case of the tertiary occupations. In their essence and in their bearing on the national economy, the various tertiary occupations cannot possibly form a single and a separate category, since, in these respects, they differ more amongst themselves than they do in combination from the various secondary or primary occupations. Yet the statisticians and the economists insist on treating the distinction between industries and services as a real and a clear-cut demarcation of economic realities.

This particular 'realist' fallacy might, however, have been condoned and forgiven had it not inspired a number of questionable policies. Some of the policies thus induced have turned out to be not only questionable but positively harmful. And some of them have caused harm at one of the most sensitive points of the world economy, i.e. in relation to economic development of the poorer, under-developed nations.

The harm has come mainly from the prescription for economic growth confined solely to transfers of resources from primary occupations to secondary ones. The origin of this particular doctrine and its justification are largely historical: a badly understood lesson of England's Industrial Revolution. In its popular version, the lesson postulates that all that happened to Britain's economy in the eighteenth and early nineteenth centuries was industrialization: a process whereby manufactures grew at the expense of agriculture.

This piece of historical misconstruction – it neglects the immense development of British agriculture both before and during the Industrial Revolution – has inspired a recipe for the economic growth of under-developed territories in which growth has been similarly identified with industrialization. The country first to accept the recipe, unmitigated and undiluted, was Stalin's Russia, and under Russian inspiration it has now become the sovereign remedy Communists prescribe for all backward countries. But it is not so much the Communist example as the advice of the economists which has been responsible for the same recipe being applied equally universally and equally undiluted to India and other countries of Asia and Africa. For all their lip-service to agriculture and rural industries, the Indian planners, until very recently, devoted to industrial projects the lion's share of the country's scarce capital flow and almost the whole of its supply of intellectual and administrative talent. As a result, India has now equipped herself with a number of the most up-to-date and immensely costly (even if under-used) steel complexes and sophisticated engineering and electro-technical industries, while its agriculture remains unreformed, the country periodically undernourished, its villages poverty-stricken, and untold millions of its rural population unemployed or underemployed.

The Indian pre-1966 example has been reproduced and Indian penalties have been paid in a number of other countries. In fact Mexico has been the only great under-developed country to shake itself free of the 'realist' fallacies of sectoral classifications and to try and foster its economic development by devoting a large share of its resources to agriculture. Most of the other under-developed countries continue to follow the Economist-Communist route. Needless to say, their failure to develop faster than they have done can be put down to a number of unfavourable factors, such as the insufficiency of foreign aid, the ruinous cost of armaments, the low prices for the commodities under-developed countries produce for export. But the misuse of their meagre supplies of indigenous capital and of the capital aid they received on overambitious, premature, and capital-intensive industrial projects is one of the main reasons why the poverty of the poor nations still remains largely unrelieved.

And for this misuse, the sectoral fallacy is largely to blame.

Other examples of sectoral fallacy will be found at home. None of them is more blatant or more familiar to the public than the Selective Employment Tax. Its underlying presuppositions and its avowed objects betray all the 'realist' illusions of sectoral classification and all the irrelevancies of theoretical aggregates. Its authors have apparently assumed that services, taken together, possess economic characteristics and have effects on the economy which are sufficiently common and *sui generis* clearly to differentiate them from manufacturing occupations. Yet, while in this respect the authors of SET follow the letter of Colin Clark's scheme, they have in other respects run counter to its very philosophy. For it is contrary to that philosophy to conclude that the economy would prosper more and grow faster if its services were prevented from expanding.

A plague of economists?

The authors of SET also believe that services – all services – contribute less to exports than manufacturing industries, that they are also less productive, or less able to increase their productivity by investment and technological improvements. These beliefs find no support in either experience or sense. The relative contribution which such services as the hotel industry, or City finance, make to current trade balances is greater than the relative contributions of such manufacturing industries as electrical appliances, bricks, or even coal and steel. As for productivities, it has recently been argued (by Professor Matthews and Mr Feinstein, with much evidence to support them) that the increases of productivity per head in the United Kingdom since the War could be largely accounted for by the increasing productivity of labour in the services. In respect of both exports and productivities some services and manufactures have performed better than other services and manufactures; and in all of them, some individual firms performed better than others. To group, for purposes of legislative encouragement and punishment, all services apart from all industries is to be guilty of the worst crimes of irrelevant classification.

SET's errors of excessive aggregation are equally blatant. In the first place, it assumes that factors of production (including manpower) are wholly general and unspecific, so that by reducing the employment of labour in some occupations it would automatically augment the supply of labour to other occupations. In actual fact the reservoirs of manpower available to such services as the retail trade or banking are largely self-contained and uncommunicating – with the result that the labour released from offices and shops would not easily and spontaneously flow to engineering works and building sites. But what is most surprising is that the economists, of all people, should have taken so little account of the differing elasticities of the demand for labour in different industries. So inelastic has been the demand for labour, as well as the demand for services, in the retail trade and catering and hotel business, that the sole response to SET has been to pass on to the consumer the higher costs of the labour these businesses employ and to continue to employ that labour in the same numbers as before.

However, SET is only one instance of statistical concepts misapplied. Other instances, not so well known and not so generally disliked, could be cited by the dozen. So can also be the instances of the harm done by irrelevant economic aggregations.

VI

Does it then mean that Britain's economy would have been healthier and Britain a happier country to live in had its economists been less influential than they are?

Some observers, even some economists, would be inclined to answer this question in the affirmative. Recently a company of officials and economists, taking their coffee at the Reform Club, were provoked by the sight of a group of government economists, filing out of the luncheon room, to try and fit them with a collective noun. Naturally enough 'a pride of professors', 'a school of specialists', 'a gaggle of experts' were suggested. But the collective noun which found most support was 'a plague of economists'. In my view the implied opprobrium is excessive. As I have already suggested, the function which the advice of economists can and must perform, even if cautionary in the main, is still very important and cannot be dispensed with. Moreover, their function sometimes transcends their professional qualifications. Such is the nature of the subject and of the academic training it requires, that it is difficult nowadays to be a good economist without also being an intelligent person. Many an economist in the government service is therefore able to do good simply by being sensible in a non-professional way. On issues which might otherwise have been decided by the rule of thumb, traditional thinking, and muddle-headed *non sequitur*, economists can very frequently be relied upon to be rational and coherent. The incipient swing among economists towards the micro-economic problems of government might be a sign of their being after all a collection of sensible men.

If so, the evil of economic advice in post-war Britain may turn out to have been not only less lethal than a plague, but also less endemic, more *passagère*. In which case 'a catarrh of economists' is perhaps a better appellation.

POSTSCRIPT

My article was written some time before the recent devaluation of the pound, but the manner in which the devaluation was presented to the public and in which it was discussed among the *cognoscenti* bears out the article's main contention. Devaluation may always have been desirable, and the circumstances of 16–18 November 1967 may have made it inevitable. But all through these hectic days the probable consequences of devaluation were discussed wholly in global terms, above all in those of exports and imports as a whole. In actual fact the effect on export prices will probably differ from very little in the case of motor vehicles or woollens to possibly as much as 6 or 8 per cent in the case of some chemicals or man-made fibres. The effect of the devaluation on the British exports as a whole would, therefore, depend mainly on the relative shares of individual goods in the total flow of British exports, and on the responsiveness of foreign markets for individual commodities to price reductions of these small and varying magnitudes. Had the problems been so conceived, the forecasts of what the devaluation could achieve might have differed somewhat from those current now. Above all, the object of economic policy in the coming months would have been not an indiscriminate switch of resources from all industries serving the home market to all and every export industry, but selective shifts from some 'home-market' industries to the exports most likely to react favourably to devaluation. And, in any case, is it mainly a question of resource available to industries, not one of labour costs, salesmanship, design, workmanship and inspection?

Mr Callaghan has wisely emphasized that the devaluation could do no more than provide a breathing space for more fundamental 'structural' changes in the economy. But even if Mr Callaghan and his department have decided what these changes should be, do his economists know them? And if they do, why has their knowledge, or even their discussion, of them been so successfully concealed from public gaze?...

9

THE USES AND ABUSES OF
ECONOMICS[1]

I

My article in the January issue of *Encounter* obviously invited a lively and even an angry come-back. To have given voice to well-concealed doubts about a group of academic neighbours is provocative enough; but what must have aggravated the provocation is that the group's own view of itself happens to be highly neurotic. It is well known for its high opinion of its intellectual status, but is at the same time suspected of a conspiratorial, augur-like, awareness of its inadequacies. I was therefore prepared for the response to be suitably aggressive. In the event it has turned out to be pleasantly disappointing. With the exception of a characteristically brash article in the *New Statesman*, most published comments and private reactions, both by letter and by word of mouth, have been more moderate and understanding than I had the right to expect.

Indeed some of the responses to my articles have carried their apparent support to a length which I, for one, find embarrassing. Mr Peter Wiles's disenchantment with current policies extends to the Western economy as a whole. His cure for Britain's ills is to subject foreign trade and payments to a regimen of quotas and allocations *à la Russe*. I trust that remedies as desperate as this will never be part of the British pharmacopoeia. An occasional imposition of what is euphemistically called 'physical controls' may at times be inescapable, but directed trade as a permanent feature of British economy is a condition more morbid than the one Mr Peter Wiles is trying to cure. People like myself would rather languish in an England incapable of fast growth than prosper with the help of 'Stalin's sterling'.

Equally unacceptable is the diametrically opposite position into which the author of the leading article in *The Times Literary Supplement* of 24 May 1968 has chosen to fit my criticism of the economists. The writer obviously belongs to the same chapel of worshippers of *laissez-faire* as Morgenstern or Hayek or Jewkes, and like them has nothing but contempt

---

[1] First published in *Encounter*, September 1968. For the contributions of Mr Wiles, Professor Beloff, Professor Johnson and Mr Stewart, see *Encounter*, June 1968.

for all attempts to interfere with the works of the economic Providence. It is therefore not surprising that he should find the true causes of Britain's predicament in socialist meddling with economic processes and in the hypertrophy of the national sectors of the economy. Few economic historians, however, will agree with him. They must rank present-day Britain, for all her difficulties, much higher – richer and better placed for expansion – than the wholly untrammelled and privately owned economy of the Victorian and Edwardian eras. For this reason alone they could not ascribe Britain's post-war ailments to the socialist proclivities of her politicians, or to these proclivities alone.

I must, above all, disassociate myself from the point of view represented by my friend Professor Max Beloff. The uninitiated may easily mistake him for a supporter of mine, albeit an extreme one. This he certainly is not. We may be co-belligerents but we are not allies. Professor Beloff holds the entire occupation of economists in contempt and wants governments to reject their counsel root and branch. Whereas I, for all my strictures, regard the economists with the greatest respect. They represent the most highly developed, perhaps the only developed, branch of the social sciences, and have a great deal of pertinent wisdom to offer to both politicians and businessmen. And as I said in my article, they also happen to be a collection of intelligent people. My objection to the counsel of economists is not that it is wholly and always wrong, but that it is so often insufficient.

To remind readers, the criticisms in my article were largely directed at the narrowly economic range of economic advice and of the public debate of economic problems. In my view the advice of the economists and their contribution to the debate do not draw fully enough upon the specialized knowledge of other social sciences or men of affairs. But the contention I pressed hardest was that within their own, purely economic, range the services of economists were excessively concerned with national aggregates and insufficiently informed with ideas about the separate components of the economy, its structural and institutional problems. My recommendations were to match. What was necessary was not to do away with the services of the economists, but to back them with the cognate expertise of other sciences and to infuse them with a larger dose of micro-economic understanding, i.e. with ideas about the influences affecting the individual factors of production, labour, capital and management, or the factors shaping the structure and behaviour of individual industries and firms.

It is for these reasons that I could not agree with Mr Beloff; and they are also the reasons for which I cannot accept and sometimes even fail to understand some of the arguments advanced against me by Professor Harry Johnson. His article consists of two halves imperfectly matched. In the first half he takes me to task for not realizing that it is in the nature of economics to concern itself with economic systems and says that my objections to the macro-economic and systemic preoccupations of economists and to their neglect of individual components of the economy betray my failure to understand the real functions of economic evidence. In the second half, however, Professor Johnson proceeds to explain why the economic advice available to the British governments is so largely made up of unbalanced and insufficiently considered macro-economic notions.

Indeed, these comments on the public performances of British economists are so uncomplimentary that I find it difficult to understand why Professor Johnson should have chosen to disagree with me. Does he not disapprove of the tendency of the British economists to 'reserve a ceremonially adequate appearance of competence...by maintaining a sporting interest in the major issues of macro-economic policy' and their habit of 'stereotyping the structure of the economy and the nature of its problems'? He goes much further than I in blaming the Keynesian revolution for the 'jettisoning not only of micro-economics, but of the broad insight into the process of economic development' and for inhibiting economists 'from investigating the extent to which macro- and micro-economic policies concerned with other objectives than the control of aggregate demand and investment have been inimical to growth'. In view of the similarities between Professor Johnson's strictures and mine, it is not surprising that his desiderata should be, or at least appear, identical with those implied in my article. His recommendation is 'to examine whether cognate social scientists on the one hand, and management and similar consultant experts on the other, have [not] more to say than the economists about what kind of changes in the existing social and institutional arrangements are capable of increasing productivity'.

Somewhat outside this stream of thought, but equally close to mine, are Professor Johnson's views of the theoretical discrimination between primary and secondary industries. In his opinion the discrimination is no longer practised by respectable economists; so that in attacking it I appear to him to be flogging a dying horse. I wish he were right! A rigid demarcation between manufactures and services is the essence of SET. A sharp distinction between primary and secondary industries – the former able, the latter unable, to provide labour reserves for economic growth – is the main theme of Professor Nicholas Kaldor's inaugural lecture. The same theme runs through several recent economic publications including Professor C. P. Kindleberger's book on economic growth in Western Europe.[1]

Even some of the contributors to the recent report of the Brookings Institution on the British economy, though exceptionally balanced and informed most of them appear to be, go on blaming the sluggishness of Britain's economic growth on the insufficient flow of recruits from agriculture.[2] Unfortunately, and unexpectedly, the worst offender proves to be Mr Edward F. Denison, the foremost American authority on economic growth. He cites with approval Professor Kindleberger's and Professor Kaldor's muddled notions about Britain's exhausted reserves of agricultural labour as an impediment to her growth; but he does not as much as mention the one-and-a-half million workers who have since the War moved from mining, textiles, the railways, domestic service and the other declining occupations into those of higher productivity. Professor Caves, the editor of the volume, in a chapter which is otherwise a model of catholicity and good sense, reproduces the argument without apparently noticing how difficult it is to reconcile with his own figures of re-allocation of employment since the War. These figures, based mainly on Sir Robert Hall's data, show that the transfer of labour into the faster growing and more productive industries went along more speedily in the United Kingdom than in the USA and, let me add, than in some much vaunted European economies.

Nothing, however, demonstrates better the continued hold of this set of statistical dogmas than the most recent pronouncements of the development economists in the United Nations Organization in Geneva. No other international official commands greater respect among economists than Dr I. Prebisch, or avails himself more freely of their services. Yet the memorandum with which he and his secretariat opened the proceedings of UNCTAD in February 1968 in New Delhi displays as clearly as can be hoofs of this allegedly dying beast. The paragraphs decrying the advantages of increased productivity in agriculture in under-developed countries might have been written by Oscar Lange twenty years ago. Lange is now

---

[1] C. P. Kindleberger, *Economic Growth in France and Britain, 1850–1950* (Harvard; Oxford, 1964).

[2] Richard E. Caves (ed.), *Britain's Economic Prospects* (The Brookings Institution, Washington; Allen & Unwin, London, 1968).

dead, but the old horse is still alive and kicking. However, what matters is not the current form of this particular mount but that both Professor Johnson and I should be now equally unwilling to ride it.

Where the disagreement between us comes out at its clearest is in the first half of the article dealing with the scope and nature of economics. Unfortunately this happens to be a topic on which I am loth to join issue with Professor Johnson. In my view a debate like the present one, conducted in general language and addressed to the wider intellectual public, is ill-suited to the methodological issue which Professor Johnson raises. Yet his argument must not remain unchallenged. So incontestable are his authority and reputation in these matters that, if uncontradicted, they may help to perpetuate what strikes me as an uncharacteristically inconsequential case.

The core of Professor Johnson's case is that it is in the nature of economics to consider the economy as a system in which individual phenomena are bound together by general relationships and that it would therefore be wrong to ask the economist [or indeed any scientist – M.M.P.] to predict and prescribe the behaviour of individual units of the system.

It would take a more expert logician than myself and a longer article than this to unravel the tangled skein of this argument. I must, however, be allowed to single out the nodal points at which the tangle is at its knottiest.

Tangle number one will be found in Professor Johnson's use of the term 'system'. If what he means by it is national economies considered in the aggregate, then what his argument ostensibly comes to is that national economies so considered make up the entire statistical universe of economics. This restriction of the subject of economics to national economies in the aggregate cannot be Professor Johnson's true object since it contradicts the many things he has written about in other places. But if it were his view, it would merely reinforce – and reinforce excessively – the reasons why economics and economists cannot be given the monopoly of guidance in economic matters. For not even the most bigoted economist would claim that there are no economic problems within ranges narrower than that of national aggregates.

Professor Johnson may, however, use the term 'system' in a more strictly epistemological sense to denote mutually related phenomena or meaningful statistical series. In this case his anxiety to restrict the activities of economists to macro-economic topics is even more difficult to understand, for both in practice and in theory macro-economic pheno-mena are not the only ones to be considered as 'systems'. In practice economists have always tried to understand the behaviour of individual factors of production – capital, labour, and entrepreneurship – not only in their interaction within entire economic systems, but also considered separately. In all these separate or 'local' studies, individual factors of production have invariably been treated as 'systems' in the second sense of Professor Johnson's term. Economists have frequently concerned themselves with economic sectors, industries, and firms within their own fields of forces or distinct from the forces which shaped the economy as a whole.

In short, economists never ceased to occupy themselves with meaning-ful studies of local and structural problems of the economy. Their micro-economic interests may of late have been overlaid by the post-Keynesian preoccupation with general theories and systemic remedies. Yet most of the existing organizations devoted to applied economics (in the first place, the National Institute of Economic and Social Research) devote themselves mainly to structural problems, above all those of individual industries and sectors of the economy. And even though in my article I singled out the neglect of micro-economic problems in the current economic debate, I also pointed out that nowadays many British econo-mists in Government offices – above all, in the DEA, the Ministry of Technology, the Board of Trade and on the Prices and Incomes Board – occupy themselves with the detailed and concrete problems of the economy. If we are to believe Mr Michael Stewart, they do so unwillingly, and even resentfully, under the Prime Minister's compulsion. But, however insufferable is their forced labour in micro-economic fields, it has helped to produce such few signs of industrial and commercial recovery as have appeared of late – in shipbuilding, in certain branches of the engineering and electronic industries. In short, it has proved possible for some economists to exercise their professional intelligence in micro-economics without ceasing to be economists.

This they have been able to do for the simple reason that in their philo-sophy economics is not restricted to 'systems' in Professor Johnson's sense of the term. Unlike him they have not as a rule assumed that national economies *in toto* are the only units of their statistical universe capable of being studied for the sake of meaningful relationships they can reveal. Factors of production taken separately, individual sectors of the economy, industries within each sector, and firms within each industry, can all be arranged into statistically observable series and exhibit their mutual relationships. Some such series and relationships have in fact occupied the attention of the most theoretical of theoreticians. One of Professor Kaldor's best-known contributions to theory deals with the economics of the firm, and so does one of the most elegant exercises (W. E. G. Salter's) in the theory of investment and innovations to come out of post-war Britain.[1]

Yet another ambiguity in Professor Johnson's argument (one of the several ambiguities he shares with Mr Stewart) attaches to his demarcation between matters micro-economic and macro-economic, the individual and the general, the theoretical and the practical. When in my article I complained of the neglect of local and individual problems by economists advising the government or participating in public debate what I had in mind was their lack of attention to the micro-economic issues, not their unwillingness to predict the doings of this or that individual firm and to interfere with it accordingly. I suspect that the reason why Professor Johnson has misunderstood me is that he does not distinguish sufficiently clearly between the generalized understanding of individual problems and the practical prescriptions for individual cases. At the cost of rubbing in the obvious, I should like to remind Professor Johnson that all theory, in fact all understanding, whether concerned with economic systems in the aggregate, or with local and particular economic phenomena, aims at revealing the generalized uniformities in statistical series or conglomerates. On the other hand most practical measures, both macro-economic and micro-economic, deal with unique phenomena. In macro-economic theories aggregate national economies are considered *seriatim* and are more or less abstracted from the individual and concrete circumstances of any particular country and time. But what macro-economists prescribe to politicians are measures to deal with individual situations – e.g. the British economy in 1968: a phenomenon as unique and as practical as any problem thrown up by any particular firm at any particular point of time in post-war Britain. In other words what Professor Johnson objects to in the 'Postanian style of individual service' is a style obligatory in *all* advisory services, i.e. in the very purposes of social engineering designed to bring generalized knowledge to bear upon individual situations.

---

[1] W. E. G. Salter, *Productivity and Technical Change* (1960).

III

I appear to detect a corresponding ambiguity in Professor Johnson's treatment of the differences between systemic and specific remedies. On these matters, however, Mr Stewart (and the writer in the *New Statesman* echoes him) is simpler, and therefore easier to discuss than Professor Johnson. I therefore propose to address this particular part of my rejoinder to him. In defending macro-economic judgments and systemic remedies in the May *Encounter*, Mr Stewart, like all other economists in this debate, has called in the marginal theory with all the certainty of a lay preacher invoking the holy writ. A holy writ it may indeed be. Even to a simple unbeliever like myself, marginal devices offer the most useful of all the tools of economic analysis. I nevertheless hope I shall not be accused of teaching my grandchildren to suck eggs if I remind Mr Stewart that marginal analysis is not equally useful in all economic situations, and that its usefulness is subject to the same limitations which most econo-mists now attach to the so-called 'production function'. Marginal analysis is most serviceable, i.e. best capable of revealing the manner whereby adjustments to economic change take place or can be brought about, when applied to the continuous ranges of commodities or resources which happen to be uniform and 'unspecific' in composition and per-fectly divisible. It is *least* useful when applied to economic systems in their entirety, or to components within them – firms, industries, economic sectors – so large and complex and so lacking in uniformity as to defy all attempts to treat them as units of a graded range. What useful aids to understanding, or what pointers to economic policy, could be got out of treating British shipbuilding – an industry of strategic importance for British exports – as *marginal*?

The position of an industry or a firm on the marginal scale will not even help to choose the proper macro-economic measures of a kind Mr Stewart favours. One can think of many general and systemic prescriptions which could for a short time have reduced the comparative costs of all British exports, including ships – a devaluation, a general subsidy for industrial wages, interest-free investment *à la Russe*. The resulting benefits, however, would not only have proved temporary, but would have differed from industry to industry and from firm to firm in accord-ance not with their position on the marginal scale but with the systemic measure chosen. Yet at the same time no marginal test and no knowledge of the industry's rank on the marginal scale would be of any help in the actual choice of the appropriate systemic measure.

Fact and relevance

Least of all could the marginal tests help economists to deal with, or even to recognize, the deep-seated causes of Britain's low and falling competitive potential abroad. The most likely effect of the marginal tests on an economist in search of deep-seated causes would be to blind his vision and to divert his attention. The troubles of the British shipbuilding industry in the mid-1960s were due to a number of economic, social and geographical factors of which their high comparative costs were merely an external manifestation. To confine the cure of British shipbuilding to a momentary scaling down of its costs with the help of devaluation (fortunately, this was not the official policy) would have been no better than doctors' attempts to treat disease by tampering with the thermometer. In all such treatments, the deep-seated causes must eventually reassert themselves and grow all the more morbid for the delay in attacking them directly.

The palliative nature of such general measures as devaluation is by implication admitted by their most passionate advocates. The advocates have sometimes recommended devaluation as a 'breathing space' – an opportunity for proceeding at greater leisure with the more fundamental structural remedies. Is there any need for me to explain that in justifying devaluation by the need to 'buy time' its advocates concede that real economic remedies cannot be wholly, or even mainly, macro-economic?

Unfortunately, a macro-economist like Mr Stewart will not be necessarily put out by a consideration of this order. Mr Stewart appears to believe that if local, specific and structural measures are required they could be brought about as mere by-products of macro-economic dispositions. He lists the possible local repercussions of general measures in a proud and loving catalogue: 'Changes in income tax affect the consumption of particular goods differently from changes in purchase tax; changes in investment grants affect the pattern and timing of investment differently from changes in interest rates; changes in expenditure by the Ministry of Housing will have very different effects on the industrial pattern of production, the regional distribution of unemployment, and even the balance of payments, from changes in expenditure by the Ministry of Social Security. And so on.'

I am afraid in a properly compiled catalogue Mr Stewart's articles of pride would merely figure as manifestations of faith. All the local consequences of macro-economic measures he lists are no more than doctrinal constructions dependent on a number of assumed and little-understood conditions. Mr Stewart's examples would have been much more telling had he been able to show to what extent his hoped-for local effects did *in fact* materialize. The little I know about them leads me to believe that most of them are no more than pies in the sky. But even if some of them could have been attained by these particular means, as mere side effects of general policies not directly addressed to them, would this in fact be the most rational, the most enduring and, above all, the most effective way of attaining them?

I suspect that the reason why Mr Stewart does not ask himself these questions is that he happens to be somewhat unclear as to where local and specific problems end and general and non-specific ones begin. The very example with which he hopes to clinch his argument, that of nurses' wages, merely reveals this lack of clarity. 'If there is a shortage of nurses . . . because nurses are underpaid', the proper remedy according to Mr Stewart, would be to raise the nurses' wages. Had Mr Stewart been more certain in his mind about his demarcations he would not have failed to discover that the remedy he favours provides the best possible example of the micro-economic and specific measures he dislikes so much in principle. The macro-economic measure appropriate to Mr Stewart's case would be to raise incomes all round by a general 'wage hike', in the expectation that the nurses' pay thus raised would satisfy the nurses and improve their recruitment. The alternative to the treatment of nurses' wages as merely marginal would be for us to investigate the peculiar occupational characteristics of the nursing profession, the particular type of labour drawn into it, and the special incentives required to stimulate its recruitment. If as a result of the investigation we came to the con-clusion that no matter what happened to be the supplies of labour in the economy as a whole, the recruitment of nurses must be stimulated and that their earnings must be raised relative to the earnings in other occupations, the sensible policy would be to lift their wages, and theirs only. And this would be the procedure and the recommendation which most people would recognize as typically micro-economic.

The logic of nurses' wages applies to all the local effects Mr Stewart expects to result from his general policies. By all means let Governments adopt general and systemic measures if and when the condition of the economy as a whole demands them; and if some of these measures also achieve desirable structural and local effects, *tant mieux*. But to expect the 'local' and structural effects to follow certainly and predictably from systemic policies would be highly credulous; and to pursue systemic policies with the express object of achieving local results would be not only credulous, but also foolish. For the local repercussions of systemic policies are bound to be indiscriminate, their costs relative to their effects are apt to be excessive, and their ability to achieve the desired results must be highly uncertain.

Indeed to rely on general and systemic measures for dealing with those problems, which happen to be 'local' and structural, is a course strikingly similar to the famous Chinese procedure for roasting pig. There are better recipes for pork joints – less costly and more certain – than the burning down of entire homes. To set a house on fire for the sake of a dinner is not only bad cooking, but also shockingly bad housekeeping.

I must, however, admit – and the admission exculpates Mr Stewart somewhat – that not all economic problems can be unambiguously classified as either wholly macro-economic or wholly micro-economic. I might perhaps have prevented a certain amount of confusion had I spoken merely of the economists' preferences for general measures, and of their occupational reluctance to re-integrate their practical propositions with the social and historical circumstances from which the underlying doctrines had been abstracted for the ease of theoretical analysis. It so happens that most macro-economic propositions are in fact presented in this disembodied form, while most micro-economic studies are evidence-bound and hence also nearer reality. This divergence of methods is not, however, universal. It is sometimes possible for macro-economic discussion to be so well integrated with social and historical experience as to disarm the most cussed of critics. Some of the ostensibly macro-economic chapters in the Brookings report fall into this fortunate category. On the other hand, it is sometimes possible for local and particular studies to be so hedged round with arbitrary and artificial assumptions as to be wholly irrelevant even though micro-economic. The recent discussions of elasticities of demand for imports, or of sensitivities of exports to prices, or of the effects of industrial structure on growth, have been cast on a scale small enough to be micro-economic; yet some of their results are little more than theory *in peto* – mere mini-dogma. To quote the admirable Professor Caves: 'Until very recently economic analysis of the relation of industrial organisation to growth and innovation has resembled theology more than science in its pre-occupation with deducing untested and conflicting general conclusions from untested *a priori* postulates.' This is, in fact, my complaint of what passes for economic knowledge and is offered as economic advice. The complaint applies mainly to systemic prescriptions, but it need not apply to them all; and it certainly does not confer the *fiat* on all the local and specific remedies coming out of the micro-economic drugstore.

10

AGRICULTURE AND ECONOMIC DEVELOPMENT: A LESSON OF HISTORY[1]

I

The subject may strike some of you as highly suspect. In a gathering so purely historical and so largely academic, I propose to discuss what I frankly avow to be the lessons of history. An aversion to such lessons has now become the occupational allergy of academic historians. If, in spite of all my fidelity to academic standards and fear of historians, I have agreed to discourse on the present subject, I have done so because I believe that in this, as in so many other respects, we, the economic species of historians, are not like the other species. Most of our topics are problem-oriented. We choose them, not because they might help us to paint in a few economic facts into this or that historical picture but because they happen to be relevant to certain general problems. By definition, general problems are problems which occur in more than one historical situation, and of which the solutions are transferable from one historical situation to another.

In fact our work is riddled with such transfers. A subject we happen to study may on the face of it be limited to a date or a place, but it is almost invariably involved with other dates and other places. To cite an author whom I do not habitually cite with any approval, we often treat situations separate in time and space as philosophically or logically contemporaneous. It is logical contemporaneity that permits us in our studies of English population in the thirteenth or the eighteenth century to draw upon demographic evidence of India in the nineteenth century or that of Sweden in the seventeenth or early eighteenth centuries; or to look to the American experience in the early nineteenth century for evidence on productivity and technological change in modern Europe; or to be reminded of England in the sixteenth and seventeenth centuries while reflecting on life and labour in China in the inter-war period.

[1] Presidential address at the Conference of the International Association of Economic History in Aix-en-Provence in 1962, published in the Transactions of the Conference, Paris, 1965.

However, what justifies me in my today's exercise is that the lessons I propose to offer are in some ways anti-lessons. By refusing to connect the evidence of the past with the discussion of today, the economic historian does not thereby banish all such connections; all he does is merely to abandon them to non-historians. This is perhaps one of the reasons why modern economic and sociological debate is crowded with questionable deductions from past experiences. These deductions are not always offered as historical propositions, but they are nevertheless inferences from what certain non-historians have understood or misunderstood to have been the evidence of history.

Some of these inferences, above all those underlying the philosophy of foreign aid (such as the hypothesis that economic prosperity breeds social peace and political contentment), are so patently naive, or else so nebulous, that we as historians need not bother much about either refuting or confirming them. Others, such as the current correlation between economic performance and educational progress, or between the rate of investment and economic productivity, are so obvious and true that they will not be much improved by further historical enquiry. But many of the current quasi-historical propositions call for further enquiry precisely because they are neither wholly wrong nor wholly right. They have just sufficient basis in historical experience not to be rejected out of hand, yet they are too crude and indiscriminate to be wholly acceptable. It is this category of half-truths that will benefit most from our attention.

II

My own interest and knowledge are too limited for me to attempt anything like a survey of all such topics. What I propose to do instead is to select as an example one proposition which figures prominently in modern discussion, namely the place of agriculture in economic growth. And even this proposition is more than I can deal with fully in a public address. In the forty minutes I have allowed myself I can offer you nothing more than a mere mnemonic exercise: to jog your memories about certain well-known facts of economic history.

I presume you are all familiar with the current views on the subject. I do not think I shall falsify them if I lump together and describe them as the very opposite of those which Mr Gelfat recently called 'agro-centric'. If a reciprocal term is to be coined to describe them it should be 'agro-fugal'. To a greater or less degree most current models of economic development identify economic development with industrialization. They all agree that if economic development aims at the rapid increase in the national product *per capita*, it cannot be achieved except by channelling the bulk of new investment and technological effort into industry and by transferring population from agriculture to manufacturing trades.

Now occasionally this doctrine is impelled by considerations which are purely ideological and military and need not concern us here. Nor need we concern ourselves with the policies of industrialization motivated by national prestige. Considered as a badge, a cockade of a nation's pride, a steel complex is far more effective than a ten per cent increase in agricultural output, and there is little an economic historian or an economist can say about this, or any other, form of conspicuous national consumption. In general, however, most of the reasons which people advance in favour of the overwhelming emphasis on industry are economic, and most of the economic reasons are historical.

The form under which this argument is commonly presented is that of the classification of occupations into primary, secondary and tertiary. Colin Clark, in his *Conditions of Economic Progress*, has done more than anyone else to give currency to the notion that the income in the primary occupations (mainly agriculture and extracting industries) is always lower than in the secondary and tertiary occupations. From this classification it naturally follows that in order to attain the main purpose of economic development, which is higher income per head, it is necessary in periods of planned growth to channel into industry the bulk of disposable resources.

This is not the occasion and I am not the person to deal with the purely statistical and theoretical truth of these agro-fugal theories. I may perhaps go so far as to remind you that the crying-up of tertiary occupations, which put nations like pre-war Rumania with her large armies and swollen bureaucracies near the top of the table, has always struck a number of critics as very odd. Some curious oddities might also result from the indiscriminate lumping of all agricultural occupations for comparison with all industrial occupations similarly lumped.

Of course in the more discriminating and sophisticated variants of the Colin Clark scheme the comparison of the primary, secondary and tertiary occupations is drawn not in terms of average incomes, but in terms of marginal ones. But here Mr Colin Clark himself has in two recent papers pointed out that when it comes to marginal productivity the transfer of marginal units of labour from agriculture to industry might lower national product in countries like Denmark or New Zealand; and his figures suggest that it might not result in any appreciable gain in Belgium, and even Great Britain.

However, all these arguments are outside my scope and competence. What we are concerned with here are the historical assumptions, and these are so obvious and so familiar that I almost feel like apologizing for rubbing them in. Since the eighteenth century in almost every advanced or advancing economy, the share of agriculture in total national product has declined. So has also the relative proportion and the absolute numbers of population engaged in agriculture. The process has manifested itself most clearly in western countries since the war. Since 1948, as national output in western countries has soared, so has agricultural employment dwindled. In fact all the current recipes for continued economic growth in western Europe are composed in the hope that agricultural employment will go on declining. The historical lesson thus appears to be largely true and well learned.

From what I have already said about the half-truths and from what I am going to say presently, it obviously follows that I also regard this particular lesson as being true to some extent, i.e. in some circumstances and at some times. The circumstances and the times are, however, all important. They must be defined, assessed if you will; and the only way of assessing them is by enquiring how the recipe worked in the past.

This inquiry I am going to confine mainly to the English example, because it happens to be the one I am least ignorant of; because it comes first chronologically; but mainly because it happens to cover a great stretch of time and a great variety of experiences. I hope you will not accuse me of piling truism upon truism if I remind you that the development of English agriculture promoted or retarded the development of the economy as a whole in a variety of ways, differing in their effects from time to time.

The timing of English agrarian development as a whole has recently received special publicity – for it figures very prominently among Rostow's pre-conditions – but long before Walt Rostow every schoolboy preparing the stock answer to a stock examination question learnt that in England the agricultural revolution preceded the industrial revolution proper. However far back you push the beginning of England's industrialization you cannot avoid the simple chronological fact that the revolutionary spurt in English economic development in the second half of the eighteenth century was preceded, *ergo* prepared, by a century of agricultural growth, of greatly increased agricultural investment, accelerated progress of agrarian technology and expanded agricultural productivity and incomes.

However, taking the agricultural revolution as a single phenomenon and treating it as a single pre-condition of the industrial revolution, would perhaps be too wholesale a procedure to follow. Looked at more closely the agrarian revolution contributed to the industrial one in several ways; it was not one but a whole packet of pre-conditions.

If you will allow me to classify and enumerate these pre-conditions, I shall list them in approximately three categories. First came food. The agricultural revolution offered the food supplies necessary to sustain the demographic expansion and to nourish the growing urban population. The second was internal markets. At a time when agriculture still employed, directly or indirectly, the greater part of the nation, the increased production and rising income of the agricultural population expanded the domestic market for industrial goods, in the same way in which the growing industrial population created an ever-expanding market for agricultural produce. Finally came the supply of labour. With the increasing productivity of agriculture more and more labour was made available for employment in industry.

These various contributions of agriculture to England's economic development make between them a fairly full assortment – a fairly full but not perhaps a complete set. Some other countries in their economic development benefited from at least one further experience in which England could not share. In countries capable of producing regular and abundant agricultural surpluses the export of agricultural produce did much to initiate and support the expansion of the economy as a whole. Russia is a classical instance of a country whose economic development and whose industrialization was for a long time sustained by large and growing agricultural exports. But for the expansion of agricultural production between 1906 and 1916 – and but for the system of taxation specially devised for the purpose – Russia's remarkable industrial progress in that decade would have been impossible. The same is, of course, in some measure true of Soviet industrialization under the first two plans, except that in that period the circumstances were, to put it mildly, too special to permit us grouping Stalin's collectivization with the more spontaneous economic processes elsewhere.

A more orthodox case of a country with agricultural surpluses in the nineteenth century is perhaps the USA. America's exports of cotton and grain in the sixties greatly helped to finance the making of her great railway system and indirectly also of her heavy industry and was thus one of the motive forces in that crucial phase in her industrialization.

I hesitate, however, to include in this category all the tropical and sub-tropical plantation economies. Some of them, while expanding their exports, failed to industrialize and sometimes even failed to raise appreciably their average *per capita* incomes. I do not want to plunge into discussion of a subject which could be discussed more expertly by the historians of 'colonial' regions, but I hope you will allow me to suggest here that the failure of some colonial economies to develop more fully was due only in part to the peculiarities of plantation ownership and control. I suspect that the failure was largely due to the relation or lack of relation of certain plantation economies to the indigenous society. Except where the peasant economy was infected by the new plantation products (as in certain rubber regions of Malaya, or cocoa-bean regions of Africa) the wealth created in and by the plantations did not as a rule spill over far beyond the range of its immediate contacts. It washed over the economy without irrigating it, or to cite a Russian proverb in a manner which has now become fashionable – the drink merely wetted the moustache without getting into the mouth.

These, however, are special cases. Plantation economies of this type should not be classified as countries with growing agriculture but should be grouped with under-developed countries containing conspicuous islands of sophisticated modern industry within an unchanged and un-bettered society. In general, in countries with exportable surpluses agricultural expansion contributed most potently to economic develop-ment and should be added to my catalogue of agricultural benefits.

III

So much for our catalogue of the contributions which agricultural development in the past made to economic growth. The catalogue, however, is not so much a card-index as a collection of 'movies'. The value of this historical experience is not only in its complexity, but also in its mobility. The agricultural benefits and the conditions responsible for them did not all come at the same time, but spaced themselves out in a very significant chronological order and changed from time to time.

Agricultural development as a safeguard of food supplies was of importance in England only as long as England could, or had to, depend on domestic production. It inevitably declined in importance as and when domestic demand outgrew the output of domestic agriculture; as and when the agricultural surpluses abroad became sufficiently regular and abundant to sustain England's foreseeable future needs; and as and when income from exports became large enough to make it possible and profitable for England to import food instead of growing it.

The same is true of the domestic market. Some of my colleagues, for whose judgment I have the greatest respect, argue that from the outset it was the foreign market for cotton goods and its infinite expansibility that triggered off the great outburst of technological change and output in the English textile industries. But it is also possible to argue that the industrial revolution was both older and broader than the new cotton industry and that its progress in all its earlier phases depended on the continuous expansion of the domestic market. Yet, even if we accepted this argument, we should recognize that, eventually, the output of exportable industrial goods rose to such an extent and the proportion of population engaged in industrial pursuits grew so much that both the importance of the domestic market as a whole and of the rural market in particular became less and less essential as a factor of economic growth. We cannot date this particular turning point precisely, but I should be inclined to place it in the 1860s. For within a decade of 1860, agriculture and agricultural income greatly declined without reducing the industrial output or the growth of national income in real terms. By that time the demand of the agricultural population for industrial goods had obviously ceased to be an essential pre-condition for further economic growth.

Finally, the release of labour, the most controversial of all the benefits, had a chronology entirely its own, and became important at the very time when domestic supplies of food and rural markets had lost their importance. We hear, of course, a great deal of the way in which the expropriation of the smallholder (or 'primary accumulation' as Marx called it) during the enclosure movements proletarized England's population and thus provided industry with its labour. No student of economic history will now hold this view in all its pristine simplicity. Recent work appears to throw doubt on the very facts of the expropriation of the smallholder as well as on the link between that expropriation and supplies of labour for industry. During the initial and crucial stages of the industrial revolution, say from 1760 to 1815, the numbers of smallholders did not decline, but possibly increased. They may have declined thereafter, but in numbers much lower than the vast additions which were at that time being made to the industrial labour force. If we are to believe Professor Chambers, as I do, recruits to the industrial force came largely from among the population already living in industrial areas, and the annual increments to the industrial labour force came not from among displaced agriculturists, indeed not even from among the displaced handicraftsmen, but from the demographic increases of local population.

However, in the second half of the nineteenth century and in the twentieth, employment in agriculture steadily declined. But by that time, the economic climate of labour transfers was no longer, if it ever had been, that commonly assumed in the debate about the industrial revolution. Labour now moved from agriculture to industry not because agriculture no longer paid, because its income and productivity declined, but on the contrary because its output per man was on the rise. In England since some time in the second half of the nineteenth century, as in Canada and USA since 1918, as in western Europe now, large labour transfers from agriculture to urban occupations have been made possible by immense increases in agricultural productivity.

I hope that this brief sketch of English historical experience, supplemented by that of the food-exporting countries, will be sufficient to suggest to you what its lesson might be. The lesson is, of course, a very moderate one, but its moderation is not quite that urged on us by such sensible and well-informed economists as Nurkse, Scitovsky, or Rodan. To argue as they do that in developing economies industry and agriculture must march in step is a precept which, historically considered, appears to be both too simple and too stable. Historically considered, the spectrum line does not lie half-way between the infra-red agrofugality and the true-blue agrocentricity, but runs all along the spectrum. In fact it shifts with time and circumstance. Had I been propounding a lesson for the fully-developed economies of the West I might well have placed the line very near the infra-red extreme, and argued that, in the light of historical experience, all the current policies of agrarian defence – the English feather-bedding, the French and German *Bauernschütz*, and, above all, Dr Mansholt's social-parity formula for the European community – are historically anachronistic. They do not fit the present stage of development in which the bulk of the population is engaged in industry and in which foodstuffs are grossly over-produced and labour is over-scarce. For the same reasons the historical lesson for the countries in which agriculture is still overwhelmingly the most important pursuit, occupying the great majority of the people, must shift much nearer the agrocentric formula. In these countries the role of agriculture in economic development is not merely that of one occupation or one industry among all the others, but that of the economic and social base for industrial progress. For these countries, as for England in the eighteenth century, development of agriculture is, and must for some time remain, the source of industrial development – its *sine qua non*.

Agriculture and economic development

I believe that this historical experience could usefully illuminate certain features in the economic history of some western countries. I wish I had the time, the knowledge and the temerity to apply it to pre-war France. I must, however, deny myself this luxury and confine my didactic exercise to some of the under-developed countries of our own time, which is after all the main purpose of this paper.

Had I presented this paper 15 or even 10 years ago, I should almost certainly have addressed myself to the problems of China and Japan. This I cannot very well do in 1962. The Chinese have of late been learning their agrarian history from lessons much more effective than those a Cambridge professor can give; while Japan has now secured a place among the developed economies by procedures which might have served me even better as a starting point than the English experiences I have drawn on. To offer to Japan at the present moment a European lesson of how to base a growing industrial economy on an expanding agriculture is to invite the classical reminder of the grandmother and sucking eggs.

There are fortunately, or perhaps I should say unfortunately, a large number of other countries in the early stages of their growth and industrialization which are still equipping themselves with appropriate economic policies. These policies differ so much that no reasonable man will dare to generalize about them. I therefore propose to confine myself to one typical example of a country, a very great country, in which the bias towards industrialization has been placed with great moderation, and where agricultural development has always been meant to play a prominent part in economic growth. I have in mind, of course, India.

There is no doubt that India's economic growth is unthinkable without general industrialization. It is also certain that a country with a population and natural resources as immense as those of India must look forward to an eventual industrial system as highly developed and as complete as those of, say, USA or Russia. The debate at present concerns only the earlier phases of this process, and the issue in the debate which concerns us here today is the role to be assigned in these early phases to agriculture.

Considering the uniqueness of India's geography, her social structure, tradition and recent history, it is astonishing to discover how closely the lessons of foreign, i.e. European, agrarian history fit it. The fit, of course, is not one of realized experience, but of the potential one; not of the part agriculture has in fact played in Indian development, but of the part it could and should play if given the chance.

Fact and relevance

To begin with, there is agricultural development for food supplies. India, in spite of her agricultural progress in the last 15 years, is still an undernourished country. She is now only just approaching the position where she can provide from home production the bare minimum of calories on the FAO scale. According to official statistics the output is sufficient to provide 2,100 calories per person *per diem*. By the end of the third plan it is hoped to raise it to 2,300 calories – the FAO standard. But as in the upper ranks of Indian society consumption of food is well above this figure, the bulk of the working population must still subsist on a diet well below the bare minimum.

Then there is the question of India's foreign trade in agricultural produce. In spite of her recent increases in agricultural production which made it unnecessary for her to import food in good or average years, she may still have to import food in years of bad harvest. In addition she also possesses possibilities of exports. India has always raised large commercial crops, jute, cotton, tea, ground nuts, which have provided her with exportable surpluses. Given her present social structure, the overwhelming agrarian occupations of her people, and the low capital–output ratio of agricultural production, India could still find it easier to step up her purchasing power abroad not by exporting industrial produce, but by reducing her imports and raising her exports of foodstuffs and vegetable raw materials. Had she this year possessed a large enough surplus of rice, she could have profitably exported it to Ceylon and China, and thus not only helped to finance her own foreign purchases for the third five-year plan, but also driven home the lesson about the wise virgins and the foolish ones.

Above all there is India's domestic market. With the bulk of her population still engaged in agriculture, the purchasing power of her internal market must still be equated with the purchasing power of her rural population. Of course, up to a certain limit the increase in agricultural production will not necessarily expand the domestic market for industrial goods. For a time larger crops will go to improve the standards of nutrition without necessarily increasing the volume of disposable cash balances in the countryside and thus without materially expanding the effective demand for manufactured goods. But eventually it must do so – must because of the part which indebtedness plays in absorbing the peasants' cash balances, and because of the part which food shortages have always played in getting peasants into debt. It must also do so because sales of rural produce in towns is bound to grow. There might also be larger exportable surpluses. In fact agricultural production, especially if accompanied by industrialization, is bound to augment the effective purchasing power in the countryside.

Of all the various items in my catalogue of agricultural benefits, increased supply of labour for industry is the only one for which India need not be dependent on agricultural progress. So great is the country's unemployment, and under-employment (the Indian planning office puts the total at 17 millions, but I have seen it estimated at 30 millions), and so great, indeed so excessive, is the flow of people into towns, that the Indian manpower problem is not yet, and will not be for a long time, that of short supply. The problem is the reverse of that – it is how to occupy productively the multitudes now seeking employment. These multitudes are so vast and so greatly swollen by demographic increases that in my opinion (an opinion which I am going to re-state again later) no plan for modern industry can alone dispose of them fully in the near future. Under the second five-year plan it was expected that by the end of the plan, i.e. 1961, there would still remain a backlog of $5\frac{1}{2}$ million unemployed. In the event, the absorptive capacity of urban industry turned out to be less than hoped for, the trek to towns heavier than foreseen, with the result that 1961 ended with a backlog of $9\frac{1}{2}$ millions. Now under the third plan, the planners hope to reduce the additional backlog by 1965 to $3\frac{1}{2}$ million. I hope they will succeed, but I have strong reasons to fear they will not.

This being the part which agriculture occupies and must occupy in India's economy, it appears to me that if India's development were to be guided by historical lessons, her agriculture would require from the planners something more than mere equality of treatment with, say, the heavy industries which it now receives. It requires an attitude to agricultural development as a pre-condition of economic progress. This in its turn means devoting the earlier plans to agricultural progress. It means expanding agricultural output, areas under occupation, and rural employments of every kind sufficiently beyond the present limits, to create vast new rural markets for industrial goods, to generate exportable surpluses and to absorb the under-employed rural population. Thus and only thus would urban industrialization be firmly rooted in the economy of the country and a viable economic system be established.

This course, for all its being historical, may yet turn out to be too theoretical to be adopted whole. It may fail to take account of military and political necessities or of economic mythologies behind the present-day drive for development. No historian, certainly not myself, would expect a planner to be so impractical as to tie himself to the dictates of economic history. Yet these dictates provide us, the observers, the critics, the historians, with a rod for measuring the distance by which India's development has or has not travelled away from its historical optimum.

v

I am afraid, thus measured, the distance appears to be very great – perhaps much greater than it should be.

We must of course be fair to the Indian planners, who are men of high intelligence and the loftiest of wills. Nehru's insistence on agrarian priorities is well known. Indian planners seem fully to share it. If the memoranda of the successive plans are to be taken as the planners' confession of faith, their creed would appear to be beyond reproach. To quote the official preface to the third plan, 'agriculture has the first priority to be increased to the largest extent possible'. Elsewhere in the plan it is laid down that 'agriculture and industry are to be regarded as integral parts of the same process of development'. The voice sounds so much like the voice of Rodan – the voice we heard in his Theory of the Big Push – that I am almost inclined to give him the credit and bless him for it. But the same note was also sounded in the earlier plans. The will is obviously there.

So if the performance does not altogether match the will, the planners can rightly claim in their justification the recalcitrant nature of Indian agriculture. There is the caste system, the vested interests of village usurers-cum-cornmongers and other wealthy men, who appropriate more than their share of agricultural investment and improvement. There is also the non-rural, I should almost say the anti-rural, outlook of the educated classes. In spite of all these handicaps, total agricultural output in the last decade or so rose about 41 per cent, the output of foodstuffs by 46 per cent, and it may have risen by as much as 60 per cent since the end of the war. In good or average years India is now independent of food imports.

Yet this is patently not enough. Not enough by the most elementary nutritional tests, for, as I have already said, after fifteen years of progress the calorie intake of the working multitudes is still sub-standard. Professor Gadgil is not the only commentator to point out that the availability *per capita* of the most important food products – cereals and pulses – was no better at the end of the second plan than it was at the beginning. Nor is he the only one to point out how much has the implementation of the second plan's programme for rural industries fallen behind targets. The authors of the third plan themselves admit 'in certain districts the progress during the second plan was less than hoped, and consequently a much larger task is to be accomplished under the third plan'.

The underlying social facts look even worse than the production figures. Much has been done to add to the area of improved and irrigated land, but not enough to provide the additional rural population with holdings. The second agricultural labour inquiry has found that between 1951 and 1956 (and the same is apparently true of the period from 1956 to 1961) the percentage of fully-employed villagers has declined, and the percentage of those offering themselves for employment has risen. Rural unemployment and under-employment, though very difficult to measure, has apparently increased by a very considerable amount (this at any rate appears to be the opinion of Gadgil and Krishnan, the only authorities I know). Hence the migration to towns in excess of new posts in industry, hence also the decline of standards of life of rural labourers. Such increases in real wages as there have been appear to have been largely confined to industrial labour, especially to labour in large-scale industry. Agricultural labour may have suffered since 1951 a 10 per cent fall in its *per capita* income.

So, although Indian agricultural plans have registered successes in some directions, they have failed in many others. They have failed to find a solution of the one problem which industrialization is meant to solve, that of rural under-employment and poverty. And by failing in this they have also failed to create conditions necessary for rooting the new industrial system in the rising wealth of the rural population.

It is, of course, possible to argue that the problem could have been solved by a yet greater dose of industrialization. For it may be reasonable to deduce from the figures of the plans that if the second plan, after having created 8 million jobs, left at least 9 million unemployed, and I do not know how many, say 17 million, under-employed, the shortfall would have been largely liquidated if the number of new jobs had been doubled, or in other words the industrial targets had been raised to twice the planned heights. Similarly, if the third plan, which envisages a 70 per cent increase of industrial production, still leaves at least four and probably as many as seven or eight millions of fully unemployed (and many millions of partly unemployed), would it not be advisable to raise the increase in industrial targets from 70 to, say, 120 per cent, and thereby to take up the entire slack?

I doubt it. I have some doubts as to whether there would be sufficient managerial or technical personnel or skilled labour for increases of this magnitude. But the chief obstacle is, of course, investment. As it is, in order to realize the third plan, India will have to invest by 1965 about

18 per cent of her gross national product. If industrial targets were lifted to produce 120 per cent increase over the second plan, the investment would have to exceed 20 per cent and perhaps approach 25 per cent. And this is net investment. As it is, Indian planners have been criticized for not providing large enough allowances for maintenance and obsolescence. Even at their low planned rates, allowances for maintenance would give us a figure of gross investment somewhere round 30 per cent of national product. Furthermore if the allowances were accelerated progressively to keep pace with the increasing age and size of capital stock, as much as 35 per cent of national income might have to be saved. To find this capital from domestic resources, even by saving *à la Russe*, till the pips squeak, would not be of much avail. Not even the Russians have, as yet, discovered how to save that much of their national income, especially if, to start with, the *per capita* income is so abysmally low. And no foreign aid, be it never so generous, could possibly foot a bill so onerous.

So perhaps it might be worth inquiring into the possibilities of an alternative solution, i.e. to increase the allocation of resources to agriculture and rural industries. This may seem, at first sight, to be equivalent to a brake on industrialization, but, in fact, it need lead to nothing more nor worse than a temporary shift of emphasis away from capital-intensive to labour-intensive industries.

Had I been concerned not with agriculture but with industry I should have had something to say about the various conceptions of industrial progress, or if you wish, of philosophies of industrialization. I could think of two alternative ones – one conceived, so to speak, in depth, the other in breadth, or in a more homely language, one with a promise of jam tomorrow, the other with an offer of bread today. The latter, the broad or the bread one, would aim to turn out as soon as possible the largest amount of consumable industrial goods and employ in doing so the highest possible number of persons per given volume of available investment. The former, the deep or the jam one, would aim at the speedy attainment of what the third plan calls 'integrated industrial structure'. This, to quote the plan further, is a structure in which immediate emphasis 'has to be placed on industries such as steel, coal, electric power, machine building and chemicals. Development of these industries is an essential condition of self-reliant and self-sufficient growth.' The preamble to the plan, in expressing this variant of industrialization, goes on, however, to promise that the heavy base 'will eventually stimulate the growth of medium and small industries and expand employment both in urban and rural areas'. In fact eventually there will be jam; but, for the time being, the bulk of the industrial investment must be channelled into the so-called 'basic' industries, most of which happen to be capital-intensive.

Under the 'bread' or 'broad' system greater emphasis would be laid on precisely those industries which under the 'deep' plans would follow the previous development of the heavy base. These are mostly small, consumption-goods and labour-intensive trades. By the former way, the way chosen by the planners, the country is more certain to attain in the shortest possible time the three-star grade of a modern industrial nation. By the latter way she would satisfy soonest the people's need of jobs and goods and liberate additional resources for agricultural development.

'Additional agricultural development.' The first and superficial reading of the successive plans might suggest that there is not much room now for any such additions; that under each plan as much has in fact been put into agriculture as agriculture could take. The preamble to the third plan lays it down that 'adequate resources [are] to be provided to increase agricultural development to the highest extent feasible'. 'Whatever is feasibly practicable should be made financially possible.' And if this is an honest statement of intent, as I believe it is, you might well think, that 20 per cent of total new investment allocated under the plan for agriculture and communal projects is all that is physically practicable. This may be so, though the little I have read and heard about this limit makes me doubt it not a little. The plan provides for a threefold increase in the production of nitrogenous fertilizers, but even at that rate the consumption of fertilizers per head of agricultural population will probably be one-half of the Japanese and less than half of the Belgian. And are there any objective physical limits to the erection of fertilizer plant? The area of irrigated land is to increase to 90 million acres, or 29 per cent more than the increase under the second plan. Is this a final limit? Have we not seen preliminary estimates of further irrigation to be done under the fourth and fifth plans?

These are no mere debating questions. Real limits, social and human, to what can be done in the Indian countryside in five years there may well be. In that case the solution would lie solely in industrial progress, though even then one would have expected the plan to lean more heavily than it does on labour-intensive industries and go more easily on the capital-intensive ones. I hope, however, that this will not inevitably be the solution. If Indian development is to meet Indian needs, industrial plans and agrarian ones will have to be integrated more genuinely than they have been so far. And if this is done not only would the Indian problem be nearer solution but the solution would come in the way in which similar solutions have come in the past.

Fact and relevance

This brings me to the end of my Indian example. It is not its object to formulate advice to the Indian planners. This particular advice would by now have been pressed upon them by people capable of presenting it better and pressing it harder than an economic historian can in an address at an academic jamboree. The object of the example is merely to subject to an historical test the case of the one developing economy I happen to be particularly interested in. Even then the historical lesson is not here offered as a recipe for immediate application, but as a study in applicability of lessons.

11

TECHNOLOGICAL PROGRESS IN
POST-WAR EUROPE[1]

I

Its title notwithstanding, this essay is essentially a methodological exercise. The methods of economic history have of late provoked a great deal of controversy. The controversy, mostly American in inspiration, has centred round the relations between economic history and economic theory. As in all previous debates on this theme both sides appear to accept the case for closer links between theory and history, and both sides have also been in favour of applying to historical evidence the most rigorous procedures of modern econometrics. So plausible, indeed so incontestable, has been the pro-theoretical and pro-econometric argument that most historians participating in a debate have been inclined to pass in silence the differences between the theoretical and the historical approaches to economic problems.

The silence is much to be regretted, and I intend to break it in this essay. It is because the differences exist that economic history has been able to lay claim to a distinct intellectual physiognomy. Without them it would have had no right to separate existence. The differences are many and various and I cannot attempt to deal with all of them on this occasion. All I propose to do is to remind my readers of the one well-understood difference that appears to me most important: especially important in the study of contemporary history in which I happen to be engaged.

The intellectual procedure characteristic of economic theory is that of 'abstraction' reinforced by 'reduction'. The economists must abstract in order to remain economic. Strictly defined the range of phenomena regarded as economic by economists is much narrower than the universe of facts considered economic by the man in the street. The latter as a

---

[1] Based on chapter 6 of the author's *Economic History of Western Europe 1945–1964* (London, 1967). It was republished in a modified form as *Technological Progress in Post-War Europe*, Sir Ellis Hunter Memorial Lecture in the University of York, no. 4 (York, 1969); and subsequently enlarged and brought up to date for publication under the same title in the *Kölner Vorträge zur Sozial- und Wirtschaftsgeschichte*, under the auspices of the University of Cologne. This is in fact the version reproduced in this collection.

rule embraces everything relevant to the production and distribution of material wealth; whereas the pure economist's universe is composed only of those aspects and determinants of wealth which happen to be scarce enough to be valuable, i.e. to command a price in terms of other scarce goods. The economic theorist will therefore remove from the range of his professional discussion not only the non-material factors which happen to be mixed up with the creation and distribution of wealth but also those material phenomena which do not happen to be directly drawn into 'market' exchanges. By restricting the field of studies in this way he is able to concentrate his argument on the behaviour of markets, or on what is commonly described as supply and demand. Thus concentrated, the discussion can be given a form more rigorous and more precise than that it could possibly have taken had it embraced the entire gamut of considerations commonly invoked in non-professional discussion of material wealth.

What gives the typical economic discussion its precision and rigour is that it can proceed by a sequence of deductions from certain initial assumptions; and this facility it owes largely to its abstractions. For so simple, easily observable and presumably inescapable is the working of supply and demand that it can be used as a starting point, the basic axiom, from which the rest of the argument can be derived by a process of deductive, essentially mathematical, reasoning.

However, for the purposes of deductive argument, in economic theory as in other quasi-mathematical subjects, abstraction is not enough. The ideal deductive procedure demands not only that all factors extraneous to the chosen field of study should be removed from discussion but that even the factors relevant to it should be chosen and handled with the greatest possible economy. What this means in practice is that the perfect theoretical argument must be confined, or at least must begin with, the lowest possible number of factors. Hence the tendency among economic theoreticians to start their analysis by constructing 'models' composed of the barest minimum of variables. The ideal theoretical model is that of a simple mathematical function of two variables; and all theoretical models, however far removed from this ideal, will try and maintain, or at least start from, some such mini-variable structure.

From this point of view the procedures of history, even of economic history, are the very opposite of those of economic theory. In so far as it is the object of economic history to share in the collective enterprise of economic science, its characteristic role should be to contribute to the enterprise the very components which economic theory cannot or would not supply. If it is the theoretician's job to remove from his argument the considerations which do not happen to be 'strictly' economic, it is the historian's function to bring them back. Needless to say historians do not always consider it their business to participate in the building up of economic propositions; and some of them will consequently refuse, or not know how, to organize their inquiries round economic problems. But in so far as they do so their proper job is not to 'verify' the relevant theoretical constructions or to buttress them up with statistical proof but to restore them to their proper place in their social environment. This is what some philosophers have in mind when they speak of the 'concrete' nature of historical study. In being concrete economic history reverses the abstracting processes of economic theory.

Thus reversed the model cannot remain 'mini-variable' and the argument must also cease to be mainly deductive. In order to bring back into economic propositions the totality of social experience the historian is as a rule compelled to handle the widest possible range of factors: indeed all the factors which can be shown or thought to influence a given economic situation. His models, if they could be laid bare (few of them in fact can), would be multi-variable or even omni-variable.

Models so made up do not lend themselves to simple syllogistic treatment even if some of them can on occasions be presented in mathematical guise. The argument appropriate to multi-variable models is not that of deduction, mathematical or otherwise, but that of induction, similar to that employed in morphological and classificatory disciplines, such as biology or geology. An historian, like other practitioners of inductive reasoning, will arrive at his conclusions by 'factorizing' the situation he studies. In other words he will list all the factors entering it and, if possible, grade them in the order of their importance. Such grading may often necessitate quantitative judgments. Statistics, with its econometric refinements, must therefore be the essential tool of historical factorization. Some factors, however, do not lend themselves easily to statistical measurement. In fact some of the most powerful processes of social life, exercising the profoundest effects on economic situations, may resist all attempts at being numbered and weighed. This does not, however, remove them from the historical narrative. The historian must name them, must even try and assess them, even though the assessment may remain sadly unquantitative.

Technological change in the post-war world, when treated historically, offers a good occasion for the presentation of some such multi-variable model and for the display of 'factorizing' procedures. This is why I have chosen it for this methodological exercise. In presenting the story of technological change I shall proceed by taking up, one after another, the many and various factors behind the post-war technology. In doing so I shall try and arrange them, as far as possible, in the order of ascending importance. I may consequently find myself winding up the discussion by a reference to factors which happen to be at one and the same time the most important and the least measurable; but this will I hope help me to bring home the historian's inability to remove from his ken the unquantifiable aspects of historical reality.

II

As every schoolboy knows the post-war world has been blessed by a technical advance more widespread and rapid than at any time in the past. The manifestations of the advance a schoolboy would be best aware of are the new products which have since the war entered into everyday use. The modern aircraft industry and the modern electronic industry, most modern plastics, synthetic resins and man-made fibres are to a large extent post-war phenomena; and so are also, generally speaking, most products of the new hydro-carbon chemistry and of the petrochemical industry based on it. The civilian use of atomic power for the generation of electricity may still be in its infancy, but by the late sixties it already represented a considerable volume of investment in the USA, United Kingdom and France, and by 1964 also in Belgium, Italy, Germany and Japan. And in the mid-sixties the laser opened up new possibilities to technologists and manufacturers.

To repeat, these are highly conspicuous examples of new products known to the schoolboys; a sophisticated technological history of the modern world will also include not only hundreds of other, less obvious and less known, objects based on recent advances in applied science and technology, but also the new processes, e.g. the new ways of making old products. Steel technology, which had been dormant for several generations, has been transformed by new processes. Similarly, the cotton industry, whose technology changed little between the 1830s and the present day, has now found itself on the verge of general transformation. Even building, civil engineering and the handling of cargoes at ports – all of them trades tightly bound by traditions – have undergone rapid technological transformation.

How are we to explain this outburst of innovation? Was it an inexplicable mutation of European culture and society or can it be related to ascertainable historical factors? This question cannot be answered by invoking a simple and, above all, a single cause. To repeat what I have already said, technological change, considered historically, has reflected in its record the action of many factors. Some of the factors can be shown to have been more important than others, but few of them could be eliminated from a true explanation of technological change as it really happened. If that explanation were to be expressed in a formal model, the model would be a multi-variable one.

In considering the many factors behind the technological change in post-war Europe it would be useful to distinguish the factors of supply from those of demand. In this context supply stands for the flow – or to use the jargon of economists, the availability – of technological possibilities: new ideas, new inventions, new openings for innovation. And the proper question to ask is, why was it that the innovating possibilities were as numerous, and that the flow of new products or new processes was as abundant, as we find them in the post-war world?

In trying to answer this question we must begin with the war itself, since a great deal of modern technology dates to the second world war and served its weapons industry. Post-war aircraft, and especially their engines, stand in direct line of descent from wartime aircraft. Most of the radar and radio development of post-war years, and with it also most of modern electronic instrumentation and computer 'hardware', derive from the radar and radio development of the war years, more particularly from the apparatus conceived and developed in the Telecommunications Research Establishment in Malvern during the war years and from the electronic devices developed in the later stages of the war by firms in the USA. The modern petrochemical industry owes its development to the technology of high octane fuels required for the last generation of reciprocating aircraft engines as well as to the German and American wartime search for synthetic rubbers and synthetic petrols. And there is no need to remind the modern reader of the connection between nuclear technology and 'the bomb'.[1]

After the war the new technology continued to profit from the development of weapons, since the continued activities devoted to the design and development of weapons have frequently overflowed into general science and technology. Some of the overflow has been very direct. Airframes and air engines developed for military purposes could without much difficulty be adapted for commercial uses. The same applies to electronic instrumentation in industrial use or to the theory and engineering practice of modern cybernetics.

Military programmes have, however, had also some indirect effects.

[1] M. Postan, D. Hay and J. D. Scott, *Design and Development of Weapons* (HMSO, 1964), *passim*.

Fact and relevance

In their pursuit of military objectives, defence departments in all Western countries, and above all in the USA, have financed a great deal of research only remotely related to defence. It is therefore worth noting that in the United Kingdom the annual expenditure on research and development financed out of the defence budget which stood at some £350 million in 1966 had grown from about £177 million in 1955–6 to over £234 million at the end of the fifties and to some £265 million in 1959–64, even though its share of the total national expenditure on research and development declined from 22 per cent in the mid-fifties to about 15 per cent in the sixties. In France military expenditure on research and development, though somewhat lower, grew very fast (it had doubled between 1959 and 1962) and exceeded NF 1,800 million by 1964.[1] And, as in the United Kingdom, a large, though unmeasurable, proportion of this expenditure spilled over into objects of civilian import.

It would nevertheless be wrong to confine the survey of post-war technological projects to military preoccupations of Governments. Since 1945 European nations devoted to all kinds of non-military research larger proportions of their national products than at any other period of their history. The world has suddenly become research-conscious. In every country large firms have provided themselves with ever-expanding departments for research and development. Most trade associations, i.e. combinations of firms, have done likewise. How great and growing this expenditure became is clearly shown by the figures in Table 1.

Indeed, so high and so expanding have been the outlays – especially after 1955 – that a correlation between innovation on the one hand, and expenditure on research on the other, naturally suggests itself. Statesmen and their advisers invariably accept the correlation and prescribe higher expenditure on scientific and technological research as a recipe for technological progress and economic growth in general.

Considered over long periods of history and on a truly international scale this prescription is obviously, almost trivially, right. If somewhere and at some time men had not pursued their researches into the petroleum molecule or the conductivity of materials, the technology of petrochemicals and of transistors would never have developed as fast as it did. If Appleton had not discovered and investigated the boundary layer,

[1] *Some Factors in Economic Growth in Europe during the 1950s*, being Part 2 of *Economic Survey of Europe in 1961*, United Nations, Economic Commission for Europe (Geneva, 1964), ch. v, pp. 4ff; UN, *Economic and Social Consequences of Disarmament* (NY, 1962). Cf. also *Annual Report of the Advisory Committee on Scientific Policy 1961–62*, Cd. Paper 1920 (HMSO, 1963). For French data see also *L'Usine nouvelle* for 18 May 1961.

TABLE I. *Expenditure on research and development 1950–64**

| | 1955 | | 1959 | | 1962 | | 1964 |
	Total (m.)	% of GNP	Total (m.)	% of GNP	Total (m.)	% of GNP	% of GNP
UK	£300[a]	1·7	£478[b]	2·3	£634[c]	3·1	3·2
Netherlands	...	...	...	2·0[d]	...	...	2·8
Sweden	...	...	...	1·8	...	...	2·8
Germany	...	0·8	...	1·2	...	...	...
France	...	...	2,230 frs.	1·1[d]	3,436 frs.	1·6	2·6

* The table is based on table 1 in *Some Factors*, ch. v, brought up to 1964. The figures for 1964 are a provisional estimate.

[a] 1955–6   [b] 1958–9.   [c] 1960–2.   [d] 1960.

radar would never have been possible, and if Oliphant had not worked on the centimetre wave, the radar technology would have frozen at the point it had reached in 1941.

The correlation between research and innovation is, however, less obvious when considered in relation to individual Western countries after the war. Our Table 1 clearly shows that there was little connection between the R and D expenditure individual European countries spent and the rate at which they in fact increased their productivities and presumably innovated their economies. The expenditure in the United Kingdom as a proportion of the GNP has been higher than in any other European country and little below that of the USA; yet we are told, with some justice, that the progress of innovation in the United Kingdom has been more laggard than in USA. The next largest pro-rata expenditure has been that of the Netherlands and Sweden, yet their economic performance, and probably also their rate of industrial innovation, has by no means been faster than that of Italy or Germany. On the other hand, Germany, whose progress of innovations after 1945 has been the envy of other nations and whose rate of economic growth has accordingly been the fastest or nearly the fastest in Europe, spent before 1961 a smaller proportion of her national income on research and development than any other European country for which the relevant information is available.[1]

[1] For a critical summary of the relevant literature and issues, see Robert E. Johnston, 'Technical Progress and Innovation', *Oxford Economic Papers*, vol. 18, no. 2, July 1966, pp. 165–6, which specifies some of the dangers of using the expenditure on research and development as indices of effective technological inputs, and, above all, the danger of disregarding the differences in the productivity of research and develop-

Fact and relevance

At first sight the lesson of these figures is somewhat distorted by the role of defence projects, which has absorbed a larger proportion of research funds in the United Kingdom than, say, in Germany. Yet even if expenditure on civil research alone were counted, the share of GNP spent on research in the United Kingdom would still appear higher than in any other European country,[1] and yet her rate of industrial innovation is supposed to have been the lowest.

If these discordances have any meaning at all, they all suggest that over a period as short as that of the post-war years, expenditure on research and development and technological progress have been imperfectly related. Indeed there is very little reason why the relation should have been any closer. For one thing, the benefits of new discoveries need not be, and have not been, confined to the nations or the firms which made them. Few countries or firms within them have depended for new technological opportunities solely on their own discoveries; most of them have owed their success in innovation not only to the discovery of new products and techniques, but to the spread of existing technology or its imitation.[2] Under the existing system of licences and business links it has been possible for nations and firms to acquire from outside new designs and the practical 'know how' to go with them. The most striking example of such outside acquisitions is that of the American firm of Du Pont. This great house has for a long time ranked as the leading firm in the chemical industry; and it is known to have devoted immense resources to its own R and D. Yet a recent study has shown that at least three out of every five important new products and processes it introduced in the post-war period have been based on ideas and discoveries of other firms. On the international

ment in different environments. On this, cf. also C. Freeman, 'An Experimental International Comparison of Research Expenditure and Manpower in 1962', OECD: SR (65.31) (Paris, 1965). A more general discussion of direct effects of expenditure on R and D on growth will be found in B. R. Williams, 'Investment and Technology in Growth', *The Manchester School* (1964), pp. 68ff; C. F. Carter and B. R. Williams, *Science Industry* (London, 1959); D. L. Burn, 'Investment, Innovation and Planning in the UK', *Progress*, September 1962.

[1] See discussion of figures in Graph I in OECD, *Science, Economic Growth, and Government Policy* (Paris, 1963), p. 25. In the United Kingdom about one-half of gross national expenditure on research and development was military. The proportion of government-financed research devoted to military objects was two-thirds of total in the United Kingdom, France, and the USA, but only one-third in Germany, *ibid*. pp. 42–3.

[2] A. K. Cairncross, 'The Migration of Technology', *Factors in Economic Development* (1962), has argued that since the war obstacles of various kinds have impeded international movements of technology; however, see here below, and also C. D. Kindleberger, 'Obsolescence and Technical Change', *Papers of the Oxford Institute of Statistics*, 23, no. 3, 1961, p. 289.

TABLE 2. *Patents and licences: the balance of payments*
(US $m.)

	USA	UK	Payments to Germany	France	Italy	Japan	Total
Payments by							
USA 1964	...	21·0	10·8	11·7	2·3	5·0	...
UK 1964	81·8	...	3·4	11·7	2·2	0·3	50·8
Germany 1964	65·3	17·2	...	5·3	1·7	0·2	99·4
France 1963	59·7	11·9	7·5	...	2·0	...	81·1
Italy 1963	57·2	15·0	15·2	14·6	...	0·4	102·4
Japan 1963	84·7	11·0	12·5	3·0	1·7	...	112·9
Total receipts from the above 5 countries	348·7	76·1	49·4	46·3	9·9	5·9	
Total receipts from all countries	550·0	121·5	61·6	47·2	32·5	5·9	

and macro-economic scale the clearest example is that of Japanese industry, where, until the late fifties, technological advances were largely sustained by foreign licences, and which even in 1967 bought more new ideas and technologies abroad than any other industrial nation.[1]

The role of the imported technologies is reflected, however imperfectly, in the available data of international payments for royalties on new products and processes. The evidence of these payments is of course indirect and incomplete, but, if anything, it underestimates the international flow of technological ideas. For instance, it excludes the innovations unprotected by patents or licences or new products and processes handed over across frontiers by parent firms to their subsidiaries, or 'embodied' in exported capital equipment. Yet its very underestimates underline how great have been the international currents of new technologies and how greatly have some nations and industries depended on inventions and innovations pioneered by others.

As Table 2 so clearly demonstrates, nations have differed greatly in their willingness and ability to receive new technologies from outside. Some nations have given more than they have received. The aggregate receipts of American firms for fees and licences of this kind have greatly exceeded the sums they themselves have paid to foreign firms. In 1956 the aggregate American receipts for technological royalties and fees approached $100 million, but American payments abroad on this account were merely

[1] W. Mueller, 'The Origins of the Basic Inventions Underlying Du Pont's Main Product and Process Innovations', *The Rate and Direction of Inventive Activity* (NBER, NY, 1964).

$15 million. The American balances on this account rose steeply in the subsequent decade. By 1964 they reached $550 million per annum, whereas their payments to foreign firms in the same period ranged between $50 and $70 million per annum. By comparison, France had a steady negative balance. In 1964 French enterprises paid some $60 million to American firms as fees and royalties, but received from the USA rather less than $12 million. France's negative balance reflected not only her own niggard outlay on R and D, but the extent to which this niggardliness could be made up by borrowings from America. The same is true of Western Europe as a whole. Its balance of technological payments was heavily in the red. Between 1957 and 1961 European countries paid to the USA on the average some $175 million per annum, but received from the USA on the average not more than $41 million per annum.[1] In 1964 the United Kingdom, Germany, France and Italy paid the US firms for patents and licences $264 million, but received from the USA on the same account $45·8 million.

These figures bear witness to the American leadership in technological progress. But from the point of view of this study what is even more significant is their testimony of correlation or lack of correlation between the activity of individual nations as sources of exportable innovation and their own innovating record. Between 1963 and 1966 the United Kingdom received more from the export of innovations, and presumably had more innovations to export, than any other European nation, indeed more than any other nation other than USA: 50 per cent more than Germany and nearly four times as much as Italy. Yet the actual innovating record of British industry has been, or is supposed to be, very laggard and far behind that of both Germany and Italy. The most remarkable disproportion between home-made innovation available for export and actual progress of innovation is of course provided by Japan, whose total receipts from the export of patents and licences in 1964 was less than $6 million compared with Britain's $122 million; and yet in the current (admittedly inexact) ranking of national propensities for innovation the Japanese economy occupies the topmost position.

More positive appears to be the relation between the innovating record of nations and their willingness and ability to buy innovations from abroad. In 1964 the United Kingdom's total purchase from the USA and the other leading industrial nations (Germany, France, Italy and Japan) stood fairly high; at about $100 million – much higher than in the late

[1] OECD, *Science, Economic Growth, and Government Policy* (Paris, 1965), appendix B, tables 9 and 10.

TABLE 3. *International payments for patent licences*

	Receipts	Expenditure	Balance
West Germany			
1963	54	159	− 105
1964	66	174	− 108
1965	80	195	− 115
1966	77	201	− 124
Britain			
1964	91	95	− 4
1965	110	108	+ 2

fifties and somewhat higher than the corresponding figure for Germany (*c*. $90 million) and France (*c*. $82 million). The UK figure for 1964 was nevertheless lower than that of Italy (*c*. $103 million) and Japan (*c*. $112 million) – the two countries whose productivities and apparent technological progress rose in the early sixties very fast, probably faster than in almost any other industrial country. The most significant contrast however is that of the British and German figures for the middle sixties.

The juxtaposition of the ability to export innovations and the propensity to import them has not, of course, been as clear in the practice of individual firms as it appears in macro-economic statistics. Post-war experience shows that the firms which have spent generously on research and development have also been most prone to acquire ready-made discoveries from others. In the words of the OECD report already cited here, 'it is those who are themselves grappling with research and development problems who are best able to appreciate the advances made elsewhere'.[1]

In other words technologies purchased from outside have not been true alternatives to innovations generated by home-based researches. In a more general way the willingness of a firm to spend generously on research and development and its readiness to buy licences and to pay royalties are merely different ways of satisfying its urge to innovate. But the very mention of the urge to innovate brings up the aspect of the problem I have referred to, but not so far discussed – that of demand for new technologies.

[1] *Ibid.* p. 34; see also statement of the Federation of British Industries in *Industrial Research in Manufacturing Industry* (London, 1961), p. 50.

Fact and relevance

III

The statistics of international trade in technological ideas demonstrate that given the willingness to innovate, the propensity to do so need not have depended and has not depended mainly on the supply of new ideas and projects generated by home-based researches. In the history of innovation, the demand for new products and processes has been of at least equal importance. If a country or a firm within it has happened to be technically more advanced than others this is not merely because it has been provided by a more abundant choice of new products and methods, but also because it has been 'in the market' for innovations, or in other words, has happened to be more receptive than others to the possibilities provided by technological advances.

It is in these differing receptivities of firms, industries and countries that one of the principal problems of technological progress will be found. Why should Germany in the late nineteenth century have been thus more receptive than the contemporary England, and even more receptive in the inter-war period than in the late nineteenth century? So important were these local and historical variations in the demand for new technologies, that a story of post-war technology must occupy itself with the reasons why benefits of technological changes have been sought more eagerly after the war than before and in some post-war countries more eagerly than in others.

This is not to imply that the current economic discussion of technological progress has been wholly concentrated on the supply of technologies to the total neglect of the demand for innovation. Any such implication would be incorrect and unfair to the profession of economists. What is however undeniable is that the discussion has been very intermittent and one-sided. In so far as the demand for innovation has been considered at all, the consideration has on the whole been confined to the hard and measurable material factors or inputs; above all to investment.

Investment is undoubtedly very important. In economic studies of technological change, investment is as a rule shown to act in two ways. One is that of 'embodiment', the other is that of 'substitution'. It is now a universally accepted theoretical proposition that every new investment, be it even in replacement of existing equipment, embodies some technological improvement. If so, the countries investing at a high rate could be expected to benefit from a higher rate of 'embodied' technological advance than nations with a lower rate of investment. It can accordingly be argued with a degree of plausibility that if the rate at which the UK economy received and absorbed new technological advances has been lower than that of Germany, the difference has largely reflected the higher rate of investment in Germany and its lower rate in the UK.

Equally plausible, though somewhat more difficult to relate to historical experience, is the effect of investment on technological progress through the so-called substitution. It is commonly assumed that the proportions in which factors or inputs are employed in production are determined by their relative scarcity and prices. Where and when labour happens to be dearer or is getting dearer, while capital and with it also the supply of potential technological improvements is relatively abundant, the tendency is to replace labour by additional capital, or to enhance its productivity by higher doses of new technologies requiring further investment.

The argument is, of course, part and parcel of the intellectual tradition of economics, and comes naturally to economists; especially to those of the 'neo-classical' school. In its simpler form – linking wage levels and interest rates – it inspired T. S. Ashton's well-known argument about the great part which abundance of capital and low rates of interest played in bringing on the English Industrial Revolution of the eighteenth century. It also underlies Habakkuk's demonstration of how scarce labour, high wages and relatively plentiful capital accounted for the greater investment and more rapid technological progress in American industry. In its more sophisticated form the explanation invokes not changes in average rates of wages and the market rate of interest, but the differences between changes in the cost of labour in a given industry and the changing costs of the capital equipment it employs or could employ if it wished; and most economists will find it also highly plausible.

Yet for all its plausibility and popularity with economists, the argument, whether in its simple or its sophisticated form, is less conclusive than it might at first sight appear. Its underlying theoretical assumption is that of the 'production function' wherein the factors of production are taken to be complementary and substitutable. Not all economists share this assumption or share it in full; and it is not for mere economic historians to question. What they must, however, question is the evidence as far as it is relevant to our problem; and the evidence is, to say the least, uncertain. Most uncertain is the evidence of relative costs of labour and capital goods. American data for 1940–50 reveal a clear gap between the rapidly rising real wages and the slowly increasing prices of plant and equipment, but European evidence, especially over longer periods, is much less certain. In the United Kingdom both wages and prices of capital goods were all but stationary between 1900 and 1914. After the violent disturbances of the war years both series settled again to a very much similar trend which continued until the outbreak of the Second World War. The index of wages (with those of 1958 at 100) rose in the inter-war years from 32 in 1924 to 34 in 1938, while the price index for capital goods rose from 26 to 28; and both series sagged a little in the middle decade. They rose violently and, on the whole, concomitantly during the second war and the first year of peace. Between 1946 and 1958 both the indices of wages and prices of capital goods rose in roughly the same degree; wages from 55 to 100, prices from 54 to 100, with prices growing somewhat faster before 1953, wages somewhat faster thereafter. It was only between 1958 and 1964 that the two trends parted company; the index of prices of capital goods rose from 100 to 109, while wages rose from 100 to 120. In some European countries, however, e.g. Germany and Sweden, the disparity may have appeared even later – perhaps as late as the 1960s.[1]

The conflict between the American and the United Kingdom evidence may in part explain why investment in innovations has been so much higher in the USA. But investment has been high also in the United Kingdom, where it has been much higher in the inter-war years than before 1914, and higher still in the ten years after 1946, even though throughout this period wages and prices moved in step.

Thus for the relative prices of capital goods and labour, the evidence is highly ambiguous to say the least. Yet even if it were clearer and more unanimous than it is, it would still remain somewhat irrelevant to the problem of post-war technological progress, as would also the simpler evidence of rates of interest and wages. By definition the relative levels of interest and wages could affect only technological improvement in established industries and lines of production capable of being reorganized by changes in the proportions of inputs. But we have already seen that many striking advances in post-war technology occurred in wholly new industries based on such new products as plastics, petrochemicals and electronic instruments, or in such new services as air travel or television. Moreover even within the restricted range of industries and products able to benefit from the substitution of capital for labour, changes in the relative costs of the two inputs would not accord with the way in which technological progress actually varied from one country to another, from one period to another and from one industrial sector to another.

The most obvious discordances are, so to speak, those of geographical

---

[1] *The British Economy: Key Statistics, 1900 and 1964*, table C. The theory of relative factor costs in its sophisticated version does not now command unanimous agreement. Cf. *Some Factors*, ch. IV, p. 16: 'There is little reason to believe that the relative prices of capital goods exerted a major influence on investment decision.'

and national incidence. If technological progress in Western Europe were so greatly dependent on the prevailing rates of interest and wages, we should expect it to manifest itself most in countries like the United Kingdom, Belgium and Switzerland, where until 1964 capital was more abundant and interest was on the whole lower than in other European countries, or in France before 1958, or in Sweden in the late fifties and the early sixties where wages were relatively higher or were rising faster than elsewhere in Europe. For the same reason additions to fixed capital in substitution for labour should have been smallest in Germany before 1960 or Italy before 1962. In these periods in both countries supplies of capital were short, rates of interest high, while supplies of labour were relatively abundant and wages rose more gently than elsewhere.

More significant still is the divergence between the incidence of post-war innovations and the logic of theory in its more sophisticated version. If this variant of the theory held good, and the costs of capital equipment compared to those of labour were the most important influence behind the varying pace of innovation, investment in innovation should have been relatively laggard in the chemical and petrochemical industries, in oil refining or in the generation of electricty. For in these branches of the economy the quotient of labour costs is very low while capital equipment consists to a very large extent of costly buildings and sites and 'bespoke' or 'custom-built' installations supplied by makers of plant and machinery least likely to benefit from rapidly rising productivity in capital goods industries.

One of the reasons why the 'objective' factor-cost argument about technological changes fails to fit the facts is its scale. In the form in which it has so far been presented here it has been concerned with national economies as wholes. There is, however, every reason for arguing that, in considering technological change, the proper unit and the proper universe of discourse should be not the national economy, and not even entire sectors of the economy or industries considered as wholes, but individual firms within them. Certain much-cited statistics of the American iron-and-steel industries between the wars show that before the war productivities differed more widely between the technologically most advanced firms and the technologically most backward ones within the USA, than we know them to have differed between country and country. It would therefore be legitimate to argue that if since the war productivities and rates of innovation have been higher in one nation or one industry than in another, this is mainly because in that industry or in that nation innovating firms have had a larger share of output. The inquiry into innovation must therefore be conducted not on 'macro-economic' but on 'micro-economic' lines and must resolve itself into the why and how of innovating decisions of individual firms.

Innovating decisions of firms have, in fact, drawn the attention of most recent students of technological progress; yet, here also, the economists, in obedience to the methodological necessities of their theory, have been inclined to concentrate on the same 'objective' factors which figure in macro-economic discussions. The prevailing assumption has been that in deciding whether to adopt or not to adopt new products or new techniques individual firms respond to the relevant price indicators – mainly those of labour and capital. This, at any rate, is the framework of the very cogent model of technological change recently constructed by Dr Salter. In his model, the decisions of firms to adopt the 'best' technique – the timing of the decision and the choice of the technique deemed 'best' – are in the final resort dependent on the relative cost of capital and labour in terms of prices for its output.[1]

There is no doubt that these three economic variables – cost of capital, cost of labour and prices of the firm's products – come, or at least should come, into consideration every time a firm decides how much of its technology should be changed or changed at all. Yet it is very doubtful whether on historical evidence, or on purely *a priori* grounds, we can take it for granted that a firm inquiring into the pros and cons of a technological innovation would find the answer to its problems clearly and firmly located at the one point determined for it by the relative costs of its factors and the prices for its products. However willing a firm might be to resolve its problems of innovation on these terms it would still be faced not with one, the perfect, solution, but with a vast range of equivalent solutions: not the one and only 'best' practice but an assortment of good practices. At the time when a firm trading in competitive conditions plans an innovation, the costs of labour and the 'notional' rate of interest are the only variables it can take 'as given' and as not influenced by the way its own decisions would go. On the other hand, the prices of its products and the scale of its sales and outputs would still lie in the future, would partly depend on its own innovating decisions and would, for this and other reasons, remain highly indeterminable and speculative. Similarly, its calculation of capital costs would depend not only on the assumed rates of interest but also on the life of the new equipment, and this, in its turn, would hinge on the planners' own anticipation and intentions as to the future rate of technical progress and obsolescence. So wide would therefore be the firm's choice that in

[1] W. E. G. Salter, *Productivity and Technical Change* (Cambridge, 1960), esp. p. 37.

the end the decision whether to innovate or not to innovate, and what degree of innovation to adopt, would depend not on what 'objectively' turns out to be the 'best' technique, but on inclinations, predilections, judgment and competence of the men making the decision, and the climate of opinion and policy in which they operate.

IV

In this way the action of the material factors of technological progress within the micro-economic limits of individual firms can be shown to have been conditioned by the social and human conditions of economic activity – the behaviour of men, their judgment and motivation, and the social milieu in which they operate. These 'residual' factors of technological progress have not of course operated solely on the micro-econometric scale – that of individual enterprises. On the contrary, in current economic discussion the social background of economic development, if considered at all, has most often been viewed in its aggregate or national dimensions. This is especially true of the manner in which such an obviously social phenomenon as the behaviour and qualities of labour has been treated by economists.

Quality of labour as a condition of economic development in general and of technological progress in particular lends itself well to generalized, macro-social, treatment; and the economists and sociologists who have thus treated it have been able to list a number of influences affecting the qualities and attitudes of the labour force. Among these influences, that of education has drawn most of the social scientists' attention. Indeed, in so far as technological progress is conducive to higher productivities and can be measured by them, the effects of education are not only more obvious than the effects of other influences, but also lend themselves better to some sort of quantitative evaluation. American econometricians have in recent years made several attempts to assign precise numerical values to the part that education has played in promoting higher productivity and have all come out with impressively high figures.[1] These figures and their direct relevance to the nations' ability to innovate must not of

[1] E. F. Denison (ed.), *Why Growth Rates Differ* (The Brookings Institution, Washington, DC, 1957), ch. 8, especially tables 8-4, 8-6 and 8-7. In all these tables the British 'Educational Quality' Indexes are the highest in Europe, except on some reckonings for Norway and the Netherlands. Cf. also *idem, The Sources of Economic Growth in the U.S.A. and the Alternative Before Us*, Council for Economic Development (NY, 1962), pp. 244–5; also *idem* in *The Residual Factor and Economic Growth* (OECD, Paris, 1964), pp. 13–66.

course be taken too literally. But taken loosely, as mere indications of underlying reality, they undoubtedly provide support to what historians have always known or assumed – that in the past better education fostered economic growth, and that greater willingness and ability to absorb new technologies has been fostered by education.

The *a priori* reasons why better education should have favoured technological progress are too obvious to need 'rubbing in'. Modern technology requires a flow of university-trained engineers and industrial scientists and of technically trained cadres in the lower ranks of industrial employment. Machines and plant in most modern industries have to be served by men able to follow technical manuals and blueprints and familiar with fundamental principles of engineering, physics and chemistry. Even more important and more general are the diffused needs for educated industrial manpower. The recourse to literate and articulate forms of communication is now greater, and so is also the reliance on book-fed rationality. For these and other reasons there has been a growing emphasis on intellectual standards in the selection and promotion of personnel.

In a more distant historical perspective superior technological and industrial education can easily be shown to have underlain the technological progress of Western nations. Historians have taught us to ascribe the technological advances of German industry in the nineteenth and twentieth centuries to the high quality of the educational system and of technical training in that country. They have also demonstrated how much Japan's remarkable industrial and technological progress since the 1880s owed to her equally remarkable achievements in popular education. A similar, though a somewhat more recent, historical lesson has been provided by Sweden and Switzerland. The high technological standards of their industries – chemical, electrical, and engineering – is reputed to owe a great deal to the excellence of their school systems, and above all to the high quality of their technical schools or colleges.

This long-term evidence finds some obvious support in the evidence of post-war Europe. European productivity and the underlying improvements in technology have grown, and so have also the supplies of educated men and women. The implied connection appears at its clearest in relation to university-trained engineers and to the national expenditure on education. Our evidence clearly indicates that in Western Europe, taken as a whole, and in most countries within it, the supplies of engineers greatly increased after 1946.

In the countries for which the figures for the numbers of engineers are available for more than one year, i.e. Belgium, Sweden and the United

Kingdom, they grew relatively to the total labour force as a whole even over periods as short as three years. Other figures at our disposal, not tabulated here, also show that in the period between 1954 and 1963 these numbers in France and the United Kingdom may have grown by nearly 25 per cent.

Even more eloquent are the figures relating to the general educational progress. European nations have devoted ever-greater proportions of their incomes to popular education; and it is consequently difficult not to conclude that the mounting output of Europe's educational establishments must have had something to do with the progress of industrial technology and innovation in general.

This, however, is as far as our evidence will take us. It brings out the connection between better education and technological progress in Western Europe as a whole and over the period of the last half-century or so, but cannot unfortunately provide a convincing explanation of national differences in technological progress in the post-war years.

Our evidence may, of course, be at fault. The figures of university-trained engineers do not mean the same thing for every country. Similarly, statistics of state expenditure on education are less communicative than they appear to be at first sight, since the content and quality of education in individual countries differs in a variety of ways not reflected in their costs.

It is, however, doubtful whether even more perfect and fully comparable statistical data would have been able to establish a clear relation between technological progress in the individual countries of post-war Europe and the standards of their education, even their technical education. Measured as a proportion of the total labour force, the supply of fully qualified engineers has not differed from country to country in a manner related to their industrial and technological achievements. It has been highest in Norway, France and Switzerland, and somewhat higher in Great Britain than either in Germany or in Sweden. Yet these two countries have enjoyed the highest reputation for the technological excellence of their industries and for their innovating propensities. Perhaps there is a higher correlation between innovation and the supply of lower ranks of technical personnel, but our evidence about the latter is too scanty to permit any statistical or historical generalization.

The correlation with expenditures on general education is no closer or clearer. In 1955 expenditure on education, measured both per head of population and as a proportion of GNP, was higher in the United Kingdom than in Germany. The gap apparently widened by 1960, though it has narrowed somewhat between 1961 and 1966. Moreover, since British outlay on education had begun to approach the German early in the thirties, the bulk of industrial labour force in the two countries, i.e. most men and women under the age of 45 employed in 1963, should have benefited from approximately equal educational provision.[1]

Other, more direct, measurements of educational progress since the war tell the same story. In nearly all the countries educational standards have risen in response to greater expenditure: more children and young persons go to school, and those who go are better provided for than in previous generations. But although all European countries have shared in this progress, the differences in its pace do not in any obvious way match up with economic performances. On almost all these counts popular education in the United Kingdom has progressed farther and faster since 1945, or indeed since 1920, than elsewhere in Europe. On some counts the Belgian record is almost equally good, while in some respects that of Norway and the Netherlands is even better. On the other hand the record of Germany and Sweden before 1960 or even 1964, was rather low. Thus the number of years of compulsory education increased in the same period from 8 to 9 in Germany, from 7 to 8 in Sweden. The latter was also the figure for the Netherlands and France in the early 1960s. The pupil-teacher ratios in the under-11 age group has improved everywhere, but at uneven rates. In Germany in the early sixties they were 80 per thousand for the lower age group and 18 per thousand for the higher age group compared with 95 and 32 in Belgium. The corresponding ratios in the United Kingdom in the same period were somewhat higher than in Germany though marginally lower than in Belgium.[2]

Roughly the same conclusion – or perhaps lack of conclusion – emerges from the tables of the so-called Educational Quality Indexes compiled by E. F. Denison and his team at the Brookings Institution. The indexes are highly sophisticated and, perhaps, too sophisticated for our purposes, since they combine into single sets of figures the data of school years completed, that of days of education per year, and that of age of leaving school. All these tables however tell a largely similar tale: and the Denison figures cited below show how greatly relevant to our theme the tale happens to be.

In matters educational Italy, whose economic growth and technological progress were most striking, lagged badly behind all other European

---

[1] See below, Table 4. *Some Factors*, ch. v, table 77; also UNESCO, *World Handbook of Educational Organisations and Statistics*, Paris (in progress).
[2] *Some Factors*, ch. v, table 77; also UNESCO, *World Handbook of Educational Organisations and Statistics*, Paris (in progress).

TABLE 4. *Mean years of education of the labour force, by sex, 1950 and 1962*[*]

	Males		Females	
	1950	1962	1950	1962
Belgium	7·98	8·93	7·95	8·81
Denmark	7·46	7·82	7·55	7·83
France	8·09	8·65	7·89	8·51
Germany	7·93	8·24	7·95	8·19
Italy	4·23		3·89	4·88
Netherlands	8·43	9·11	8·35	9·02
Norway	7·90	8·40	7·70	8·28
UK	9·16	9·71	9·43	9·86

[*] Based on E. F. Denison, *Why Growth Rates Differ*, p. 107, table 8-12.

countries. In Germany before 1904 the education of the labour force advanced comparatively slowly. On the other hand, in the United Kingdom the index was already very high – the highest in Europe – in the fifties and, except for Belgium, retained its topmost place in the early sixties.

These figures are not cited to prove that education was not a propellant of economic progress. To repeat, in the long run, economic growth everywhere benefited, or should have benefited, from popular education. In considering the economic advances of the nineteenth and twentieth centuries or in comparing the economic achievements of Western countries with those of the 'underdeveloped' nation, it is impossible not to note the part played by spreading literacy and training. But when our attention is confined to Europe itself and does not extend beyond the postwar years, the effect of further improvements in education on economic and technological progress appears to be less obvious. In countries already possessed of modern school systems, further additions to educational expenditure, or to the educational efforts in general, may not have produced an economic or even a purely technological return as clearly observable as the 'returns' to education in more backward countries.[1]

Current discussion of labour as a factor of technological progress is not however confined to qualities imparted to it by education. Another

[1] It is one of Denison's predictions (in *Sources of Economic Growth*, see p. 135, n. 1 above) that the contribution of education to economic growth would tend to decline in the future, i.e. after its initial benefits had been realized. In his section of *The Residual Factor in Economic Growth* (OECD, Paris, 1964), pp. 46–8, Denison estimates that, as between the United Kingdom and the United States, only 3 points, out of 45 points difference in real product per head, can be ascribed to differences in education.

'quality' of the labour force commonly brought into the discussion of innovation is that of its economic deportment: its attitude to work, its behaviour on the shop floor, its social and personal relations with managers and other workers. We are thus told that in countries and periods most afflicted with unemployment, e.g. in the United Kingdom before the war, labour-saving innovations in industry were not welcome to trade unions and their rank-and-file, and that consequently the dislike of time-saving devices of modern production engineering had become part of the trade union traditions in most industries. The delays over the introduction of automatic looms into the British textile industry before the war or of new processes in the printing industry of most European countries are as a rule cited in this context. If so, it is possible that the more favourable attitude of labour-saving technology in some countries after the war may have resulted from full employment and the weakening of traditional fears of redundancy.

However, this evidence, plausible as it is on general grounds, is difficult to fit into what we know of actual international divergences in labour attitudes to innovation. Equally plausible and equally difficult to fit into the actual post-war experience in the West are the commonly assumed and much discussed international differences in the collective characteristics of working men of different nationalities. The man-in-the-street might talk glibly about the industry, sobriety and good sense of the German workers, the lack of discipline of the Italian workers, the happy-go-lucky spontaneity of negro workers and of the 'inherited skills' of the Swiss; and there is little doubt some of these commonplace generalizations are well grounded in the observations assumed and accepted as true by writers of the social and economic history of the earlier periods. Unfortunately none of these observations has been, or could be, brought to bear on differences in the innovations and productivities of the advanced industrial countries after the war.

The only aspect of post-war labour to have been thus drawn into the discussion is immigrant labour, or, as it is sometimes described, 'green' labour. Several recent writers have argued that in countries like Germany, Switzerland or France the structure of labour force has become favourable to technological progress thanks to the large numbers of immigrants. For, so the argument runs, immigrants have been more adventurous, more mobile, more acquisitive, less wedded to established routines and, for these reasons, better able to adapt themselves to new occupations and new methods. The problems of 'green labour' have been recently investigated by a Commission of OECD. In its findings, however, the

Commission has not gone much further than to conclude that the 'green labour' of recent immigrants from abroad or recruits from agriculture could be employed in industry as productively as that of industrial workers born and bred in the industrial milieu.

Thus, generally speaking, all the so-called 'qualities of labour', though generally assumed to be highly relevant to technological progress, are very difficult to link up with the higher rates of technological progress in Western Europe after the war, or with the differences in these rates between country and country. The difficulty is, of course, partly one of evidence. It is one of the worst penalties of social study that the social and psychological variables lend themselves badly to analysis and measurement. But one of the reasons why our evidence is so uncertain is that the correlation itself may be not as close as it is often thought to be. On *a priori* grounds we must assume that quality of labour is one of the social and human influences behind technological progress. But on the same *a priori* grounds we cannot expect this influence to be so overwhelming as to dominate the entire social situation. Other social and personal factors were also at work, and some of them may have been as powerful as, or even more powerful than, the qualities of labour.

Of these qualities, the most powerful may turn out to have been the quality and the behaviour of the entrepreneurs and managers. The crucial role of entrepreneurs in the progress of innovation is now generally realized and this realization underlies the true, though fashionable, proposition, that the so-called 'technological gap' is in reality a 'managerial' one. If some of the more advanced nations of the West have after the war innovated more rapidly and more successfully than others, the reason for this should be sought not only in the more plentiful supply of innovating ideas (though these might have been of some importance), but also in the greater willingness of their entrepreneurs to exploit the ideas available to them.

'Go far to explain.' Here again we must repeat our recurrent warning. However far-reaching the effects of managerial propensity to innovate, other features and qualities of management – their motivation, their recruitment, their education, their ranking in society – affected not only the willingness of entrepreneurs to innovate but also their ability to do so. More is now known about these qualities of management – especially those dependent on education and recruitment – than was known a few years ago. Yet not enough evidence has been assembled, and such evidence as has been assembled has not yet been sufficiently digested, to support a balanced historical account of the entrepreneur's role in innovation and, still less, a coherent theory of the managerial role in technological progress. Until such an account and such a theory is available we are left with mere general impression, perhaps no more than a hunch that of all the social and personal factors of innovation the behaviour of entrepreneurs and managers was possibly the most crucial, and that of all the changes that have come over industrial and commercial enterprises, those which occurred at the very top, among its leaders, mattered most. The changing qualities of character and judgment on the higher levels of managerial personnel have imprinted themselves upon the organization and the performances of enterprises whether private or public; and it is through them that the impersonal historical factors have borne upon the innovating propensities of the economy.

Of the various characteristics of entrepreneurs and managers, the one most commonly discussed and best served by historical evidence is that of entrepreneurial rationality, i.e. of the degree to which the attitude of business leaders to the methods of their businesses is based on the objective assessment of the possibilities open to them. The experience of European industry in the nineteenth and twentieth centuries will not permit the historian to assume that industrial and commercial leaders always took the decisions to innovate or not to innovate on what economists or even sociologists would accept as rational grounds. In a recent inquiry into technological progress in British industry, Professors Carter and Williams, following the hunches of their historically minded predecessors – Schumpeter, Weber, and Sombart – distinguish between firms rationally conducted and those wedded to their traditional ways. They have shown how the ability and willingness of a firm to adopt the best technological practice and re-equip itself for this purpose have depended mainly on the degree to which its management is rational. On this showing a firm's technological progress in the past depended not only on the 'objective' factor of innovation but also on the managers' ability to take 'objective' and reasonable decisions.

This historical lesson has recently been brought out anew in several inquiries into British business methods. Thus a recent report of a British commission inquiring into turnover taxation contains an implied suggestion that the heads of a number of firms were unable to understand and to measure the effects of fiscal aids to investment; an inability rooted in their rule-of-thumb methods of conducting business.[1] Similar suggestions will be found in most recent inquiries into British management.

It may well be that this particular failure has been more characteristic

---

[1] *Report of the Committee on Turnover Taxation*, Cmnd. 2300 (HMSO, 1964), p. 77.

of British managers than it would be of their contemporaries in other countries; but if true, this makes it all the more necessary to assign to these differences their full weight in an historical discussion. If the British example (and, for that matter, similar facts available for French and German industry) has any significance, it clearly indicates that the ability of firms to approach their production methods rationally and the prevalence of such firms in any given industry or country go far to explain that country's or industry's technological record.

In this way an historical account of technological change, multivariable as all such accounts are bound to be, resolves itself into an entire gamut of economic and social factors, those of supply and those of demand. All, or nearly all, these factors have had some part to play in the progress of innovation, but some have probably influenced the progress more than others. In fact the very manner in which the gamut has been displayed here has been that of ascending importance – from macro-economic conditions to the micro-economic ones, from material circumstances to the social and human ones. It is therefore not an accident that the last of the influences discussed here – that of managerial qualities – should have been the one in which the social, human and micro-economic factors of innovation combined and operated most powerfully. What a pity therefore that in the present state of our knowledge this residual combination should be not only so powerful, but also so difficult to demonstrate in clear-cut and quantifiable terms.

12

A STUDY OF HISTORY[1]

I

To review Professor Toynbee's three volumes eighteen months after
their publication is to run all the risks of delay without reaping any of its
benefits. A belated review is always in danger of becoming a mere review
of reviews, either a reflection of the earlier opinions or a revulsion from
them; and in dealing with Professor Toynbee's book the danger is only
heightened by the certainty and unanimity of the world's first opinions.
At the same time the interval has done nothing to facilitate the formation
of a final judgment. A late commentator is at as great a disadvantage now
as the prompt reviewers were a year ago, in that he still has to survey a
mere beginning of the great enterprise. Now, as a year ago, little can be
said, either in praise or in criticism, that is likely to survive the subsequent
unfolding of Professor Toynbee's design. The present essay has therefore
nothing to offer except a few reflections, some of which relate to things
said about the book rather than in the book itself, and all of which are
destined to be provisional.

The main themes of the three volumes are too well known by now to
require a detailed retelling. Professor Toynbee sets out to find in history
an explanation of the rise and growth of civilizations. Having distinguished
civilization from society, and having defined the former as the phase of
creative activity in the latter, he then proceeds to explain the appearance of
the creative phases. He dismisses the theories of race and geographical
environment in their conventional formulation. Whatever his detailed
arguments against these hypotheses (and he mostly attacks them on the
ground of their relativity and inconsistency), his real, though unexpressed,
objection to them is contained in his definition of civilization. Geography,
climate and race, treated as constants, cannot account for something which
to the author is a dynamic and transient state. The true cause must be as
dynamic as the civilization itself, and this cause Professor Toynbee finds
in 'challenge and response'. Societies are exposed to a variety of 'challenges'. Some of them come from outside: hard climate, rigours of migra-

---

[1] A review of A. Toynbee, *A Study of History*, vols. I–III (London, 1934), first published
in *The Sociological Review*, vol. XXVIII, no. 1, January 1936.

tion, poverty of the soil. Others rise from within society itself: over-population, penalization of minorities. Some are due to events in the physical world: desiccation, the spread of the forest. Others are due to human agencies: the pressure of neighbouring societies on the marches, the assimilating action of foreign cultures. But whatever its nature and origin, the challenge makes the existence of society on pre-existing terms impossible. The society must either decline and disappear or accept the challenge and adapt itself to the new conditions; and it is in accepting the challenge and in the process of responding to it that societies generate that intense form of activity which distinguishes the creative state of civilization from the passive state of mere social existence. Yet not every response to every challenge will lead a society to a civilization. Challenges can be so severe and the responses they produce so exacting that the whole of social activity is absorbed in re-establishing and maintaining social existence. In order to generate a state of true civilization the challenge must be moderate; neither too hard nor too easy. The 'Golden Mean' is the rule of the truly effective challenge and of the truly creative response.

Having thus accounted for the rise of civilizations, Professor Toynbee proceeds to the analysis of their growth. Growth to him is a discontinuous process, a sequence of disequilibria and states of balance; of old problems solved and of new problems rising on the ruins of old solutions. Yet within this series of alternating phases there is a constant progression and a direction. The reciprocal motions of a growing civilization all lead to higher forms of life and culture. In their upward climb civilizations achieve an ever greater command over environment and attain ever higher degrees of differentiation (which presumably means variety and complexity of social forms), and of etherealization (which presumably means freedom from preoccupation with the material facts of existence). For this ascent the existence of leading men and leading societies is essential, and the mechanisms of leadership, like growth itself, is a process of alternating phases, of 'withdrawal and return'. Leading societies and leading men must pass through a phase of inactivity before they are able to place themselves ahead of the others on the way to the higher levels of civilization.

These main themes, and especially that of 'challenge and response', dominate the whole of Professor Toynbee's enormous collection of evidence. The ingenuity with which they are fitted to disparate facts, drawn from an infinite variety of epochs and places, the insight and imagination which transform the detached and seemingly irrelevant facts into essential parts of a unified theory, all make the book seem unlike anything else ever written about history in the English language. Over and over again the argument is brought to the very verge of a great revelation, and over and over again the reader is made to feel that he is hot on the trail of the one and the only meaning of history.

But the chief value and the chief fascination of the book is not so much in the great expectations which its principal ideas raise, as in the facts from which they rise. The infinite wealth of fact and allusion creates a pattern as intricate and a texture as rich as those of an Oriental carpet. There is no subject in history which it does not touch, and for every subject it touches it gives a summary of the present position in scientific discussion. Thus, whether the book fails or succeeds as a philosophy of history it will always remain a concordance of history, an encyclopaedia of *Kulturgeschichte* in a non-alphabetical order. Professor Toynbee possesses the gifts of a truly great encyclopaedist, of a Diderot or a D'Alembert, for he is capable of holding and giving out essential information while pursuing an argument. It matters not that on some topics the information is slightly out of focus, or that on others the present state of knowledge is too nebulous and too yielding to be even summarized with impunity by men with a philosophic purpose. What is important is that for the first time the essentials of modern knowledge in every imaginable field of history and archaeology have been set out by a man capable of comprehending and handling them.

The book will also delight some people, as it did the reviewer, by its approach to historical evidence. Professor Toynbee does not pursue historical information for its own sake. To him historical information is a species of scientific evidence. Like the data of archaeology and anthropology, and in combination with them, the facts of history supply an empirical foundation to the science and philosophy of society. In support of this attitude Professor Toynbee adduces a number of arguments some of which will not carry conviction, but the attitude itself is sufficiently clear and sufficiently reasonable to stand, even if the supporting arguments do not. Thus, to insist that historical facts are comparable even when separated by centuries and millennia, merely because the time covered by the history of civilization is infinitesimally small relatively to the antiquity of mankind, is not very helpful or relevant, since it is not the history of mankind but the history of civilizations that Professor Toynbee has chosen for his subject. The real argument for his view will be found in the title of the chapter in which it is expounded. To have called it 'The Philosophical Contemporaneity of the Civilized Societies', is to have produced the best justification. However widely separated in time, historical evidence can be contemporaneous in meaning, i.e. in the light which it is able to throw on the constant and the unchanging elements of human society and human nature.

This attitude Professor Toynbee shares with a larger number of younger historians who regard themselves as partners in the joint enterprise of social science; and if allowed to put on his work the simplest and the most familiar of the many interpretations which it permits, they would probably find themselves in agreement not only with his attitude to historical evidence but also with the substance of his historical ideas. Simple-minded social scientists could, if they wanted, discover familiar and acceptable meanings in many of Professor Toynbee's strange-sounding words. At its simplest and most definite, 'challenge and response' may be merely a euphonious way of referring to what writers more prosaically minded have been accustomed to describe as 'effects of environment'. Biologists and sociologists and even the old-fashioned historians have been in the habit of considering the social as well as the geographical environment, and no modern definition of environment is as simple as those Professor Toynbee attacks in his discussion of race and geographical factors. In its modern connotation environment is no more (and unfortunately no less) external to the object than Professor Toynbee's 'challenge'. Nor is it always considered in a static condition. When historians and sociologists emphasize the effects of environment on the *origins* of phenomena, they cannot help considering it as a factor newly introduced, as a dramatic change and a revolutionary rearrangement of conditions. They treat the political effects of the oversea migration of the Anglo-Saxons, or the social effects of the Eskimo settlement on the Arctic icefield, in a way which differs very little from what Professor Toynbee has to say when he treats the same phenomena as 'challenges'. And in many other situations which Professor Toynbee classifies as 'challenge and response', they would recognize the old and familiar 'effects of a changing environment'.

There is a similarly familiar ring about his other inventions. His 'Golden Mean', when taken in its most sensible version, reminds one very closely of the nineteenth-century discussion of the blessings of the British climate. Professor Toynbee, like Buckle, believes in the advantages of an environment which is neither too easy nor too hard; and like Buckle he gives no other indication for identifying and locating the golden mean except as the point at which the best results occur. But however circular, the argument is familiar and simple. Equally familiar is the idea underlying Professor Toynbee's notion of growth. If taken in the simplest and the most definite of its possible meanings, it becomes yet another version of what Marxists describe as the dialectical process. Professor Toynbee compares evolution to the mechanics of walking: a mode of progression in which the body is thrown out of balance after each successive state of equipoise. The simile and the underlying concept of advance through antithetic stages would be hailed by the Leninists and Stalinists as the nearest to their own simplified rendering of Hegelian dialectic. It is somewhat more difficult to get a definite meaning out of the 'withdrawal and return', but in so far as it exists it is exceedingly plain. In one of the senses in which Professor Toynbee employs it, it appears to be an additional application of the dialectical concept. 'It is sown in dishonour, it is raised in glory; it is sown in weakness, it is raised in power.' But sometimes the author uses it to indicate something which is simpler still. Many of his examples merely demonstrate that societies and men sometimes gather forces before starting a successful enterprise, or that men must collect their thoughts before giving them out to the world. This simplest of truths is all that can be derived from his discussion of Italy's greatness in the sixteenth century after her relative insignificance in the thirteenth and the fourteenth, or of England's greatness in the nineteenth century after several centuries of relative obscurity. Neither Italy in the thirteenth century, nor England in the seventeenth, were in any real sense of the word inactive, and all that the word 'withdrawal' can mean here is that the earlier record was overshadowed by the subsequent achievements. Nor would anybody in his senses, even a child, deny the suggestion that periods of exceptional achievements are apt to be preceded by periods of which the achievements were less exceptional.

II

Thus, if all Professor Toynbee's ideas were presented and accepted in their simplest and most definite meanings, the book would, in addition to being a great encyclopaedia, become also a great sociological anthology: a magnificent collection of beautifully reproduced illustrations of the familiar ideas about the rise and growth of civilizations. But great as is our need of such a collection, and remarkable as are the gifts which Professor Toynbee brings to its selection and arrangement, there is not the slightest probability of the book being offered or read as a mere anthology of social history. It is not through accident and certainly not through ignorance that Professor Toynbee has rejected the traditional and familiar terms. He has coined new words because he has been seeking new concepts. By his new phraseology he has intended to convey a range of new meanings and a system of new ideas. It is this intention that will probably raise most doubt, for the bulk of his new inventions are too wide and too vague to lead to a true sociological discovery, while the few which happen to provide openings for a truly original and a perfectly definite enterprise are left unexplored. The width and the vague suggestiveness of most of the book's concepts are among its most conspicuous features. Over and over again the author imparts to his terms a multiplicity of new meanings by depriving them of their old clarity. A system of ideas is thus reared, which by its very vagueness offers more than it can give and excites reason beyond its power of satisfying it. And what emerges is not a new philosophy of history but a multiplicity of old philosophies muffled and veiled.

The reason why Professor Toynbee has been led to charge most of his concepts with so many vague meanings will be found in his technique of argument. The technique is that of literary metaphor. Whenever he approaches a new and a complicated concept he suddenly abandons the ordinary procedure of analysis and turns to artistic images. 'Let us shut our eyes for the moment to the formulae of science and open our ears to the language of mythology' (vol. I, p. 271); and in the language of mythology we get the contrasting images of Zeus and Prometheus, instead of an analysis and a definition of the difference between reactionary domination and creative initiative. The Chinese symbols of the Yin state and the Yang state are employed to convey the distinction between society and civilization, the simile of walking or rock-climbing to describe growth and evolution. These visual images are among the most fascinating features of the book, importing into the argument brilliant flashes of poetic vision, which appear to penetrate deeper than the dim light of mere sense. Had he used them to illustrate concepts previously defined, they would have added to the book's charm without detracting from its intellectual quality. Unfortunately, they are often used not as embellishments, but as structural parts of the arguments; not as aids to exposition, but as substitutes for thought. He reaches out for an image, not after he has succeeded in building up a logical concept, but when he is afraid that logic may fail him. 'The event can best be described in these mythological images, because they are not embarrassed by the contradiction which arises when the statement is translated into logical terms' (vol. I, p. 278). Unfortunately concrete poetic images are only too good a refuge from the embarrassments of sense. A whole regiment of loosely related meanings can camp at ease in the generous shade of a single metaphor. The author can use them all at once or one at a time, to suit the argument and to fit the example; and however scrupulous and honest his intentions (and Professor Toynbee's are irreproachable), his achievements are bound to suffer from this excess of freedom.

It is this dangerous licence of pictorial image that is responsible for the reader's difficulties with Professor Toynbee's notions of society and civilization. By a cumulative effect of simile and allusion, Professor Toynbee succeeds in creating the impression of a civilization as an active phase in the life of society, but as long as this remains a mere impression, with a scope and a meaning undefined, it affords the author a fatal freedom of operation. It enables him to employ the concept in several conflicting senses to serve the passing contingencies of his argument. Thus, if civilization means an active phase in the life of a society it cannot be exposed to challenge, transferred (vol. I, p. 334), or raise its head (vol. II, p. 79). And if civilization is activity, is it identical with the activity of responding to a challenge or is it something generated in excess of the response? And if civilization is defined as the activity of responding to a challenge, is not then the whole discussion of the challenge and response as the 'cause' of civilization somewhat tautological? And if civilization is an activity identical with a successful response, how are civilizations to be ranked, and how can successful responses be compared with each other and distinguished from those which failed? If they are to be judged by the results which they have created, and in which they stand enshrined, civilizations are at once identified with what Professor Toynbee is inclined to describe as 'cultures', which he apparently does not, himself, identify with civilizations. His introductory analysis of universal civilizations suggests that he intends to adopt for his index the degree to which a civilization approaches universality. Had he done this he would then have had to decide on the best way of measuring a deviation from the index; but he has saved himself the trouble by refusing to employ any single standard, and by using impartially an infinite variety of measures. He sometimes ranks civilizations according to a single cultural achievement, arbitrarily selected; thus we are told that the Icelandic civilization is higher than that of the Scandinavians at home, because the epic is a higher form of art than the drama. Sometimes the index is the capacity for extending over great areas (Russia from the fourteenth to the eighteenth centuries), but sometimes to succeed means only to hold the ground against a powerful political and cultural influence. Sometimes it is the capacity for repelling military aggression (Austria in the seventeenth and eighteenth centuries); sometimes it is the capacity for indulging in it (Turkey until the seventeenth century). In one case to have come to Constantinople as hall porters and commissionaires is described as a successful response to the challenge of penalization (vol. II, p. 214), and in another place readers are left wondering whether the humiliating ceremonies which the Dutch merchants had to undergo in unreformed Japan are also an instance of a Yin-activity, generated by responding to the same challenge. If any common feature at all can be discovered in the infinite variety of Professor Toynbee's successful responses, it is the one which he himself would hardly like to see put into words. A complete and impartial list of Professor Toynbee's 'successes' would be merely a list of events and situations which happen to have made sufficient splash to receive large notices in history books. Thus, in spite of the suggestive references to the German *Aufklärung* in vol. III, the one German achievement which he constantly emphasizes is not the art of the sixteenth century or the music and philosophy of the eighteenth, but the formation of the Empire in the nineteenth. Similarly, the great period of the history of Russian civilization is not her great renaissance of the nineteenth century, but her conquest of the Eurasian continent in the sixteenth, seventeenth and eighteenth. The achievement of Polish civilization is not the literary and intellectual activity of her post-partition days, but the battle of Tannenberg in 1410. In the same list medieval Hungary occupies a more important place than medieval Flanders, Venice appears greater than Florence, and of the fair land of Languedoc there is hardly a word. In short, if there is any standard at all, it is that of the Ph.D. student, who in his thesis on great men measured greatness by the size of the notices in *Who's Who*. And yet, however superficial and however unintentional, this standard is the only one by which Professor Toynbee's civilization can be appraised as an 'activity' distinct either from its 'field', i.e. the society, or from its achievement, i.e. culture, social and political organization and mode of life.

Still greater are the penalties which Professor Toynbee pays for the convenient vagueness of his concept of 'withdrawal'. So many and so different are the suggestions which the image of withdrawal carries with it that it enables and leads him to group together most ill-assorted situations. Solon becoming a merchant before returning to his native city as a law-giver, and Hamlet immersed in introspection, are both instances of withdrawal preceding a creative effort. So also is Peter the Great's journey to the West, Machiavelli's enforced retirement into a provincial town, St Paul's anti-Christian prelude, England's lack of international ties from the fifteenth to the eighteenth centuries (*sic!*), the psychological condition of puberty, Hindenburg's retirement from active service a few years before the war and again before his election to the presidency.

Professor Toynbee has utilized to the full the dangerous possibilities of his poetic method and yet he has failed to avail himself of its one and only opening for a truly scientific analysis. In one concept at least, that of 'challenge and response', the widened meaning which a literary image provides could easily have involved Professor Toynbee in a sociological inquiry. The very binomial structure of the term, the coupling of the active agent with the effects of its action, might have enabled Professor Toynbee to proceed much farther than the biologists and sociologists have so far done in abolishing the artificial abstraction of the object from the environment. The possibility has not escaped the author and is implied in his treatment of concrete examples. Forest and marshes, steppes and rivers, migration over seas and mountains, all acted both as stimuli and as soporifics in the lives of different societies. What a geographical factor or a political event turns out to be in the history of a society depends, as Professor Toynbee himself admits, on the society itself. 'Transmarine migration is merely a possible stimulus and not an automatic and infallible forcing process of mental growth, and if the stimulus provokes no response, there is little virtue in the stimulus' (vol. III, p. 135). Thus, had he responded to the challenge of his own terminology, he would have tried to bring out the factors that make a challenge challenging. He would have given us the analysis of societies challenged and would have tried to find by what social rearrangements, by what changes in their material and spiritual equipment, some societies were made to feel a certain phenomenon as a moderate challenge, while others were either not challenged by it at all, or challenged only too severely. He would also have classified responses as well as challenges, and would have analysed the mechanism of response. Why did the Assyrians fail to respond to the Scythian challenge while the Medeans succeeded? Why was the English response to the Scandinavian challenge different from that of the Irish? Why did the Zoroastrian and the Jewish societies fail while the Mohammedans succeeded in meeting the Hellenic challenge? How does the capacity for experiencing a challenge differ from the ability to respond to it successfully? Do the same social factors which determine the degree of the challenge also determine the quality of the response?

All these questions may still be answered in the subsequent volumes, and if they are, Professor Toynbee's work will automatically become a contribution to social science. The problems of challenge and response, which it so far leaves unsolved, are all sociological problems. They are sociological not only because they concern the internal structure of society, its social organization and social equipment. Even in his first three volumes, Professor Toynbee occasionally raises issues which belong to the inner structure of societies (e.g. his 'stimulus of penalization' or the social penalty of 'excessive responses' in Turkey and Sparta), without, at the same time, turning into a scientific sociologist. What makes a question sociological is not only the nature of the problem it raises, but also the nature of the answer it requires. It is the great virtue of some questions that they can only be answered in a sociological way, by the laborious and painful process of social analysis, by defining and classifying social groups and institutions, by counting and measuring the differences in social arrangements from place to place and from time to time.

Sociological treatment also involves a difference of scale. There is no objection to the scientific analysis being extended to the whole area of Professor Toynbee's field. The only objection to his scale is that it is beyond the powers of any human being, however gifted and learned. For some parts of the field the information is so scanty and so unreliable that close analysis is impossible, and for those parts of the field where facts are sufficient they are too numerous to allow any time for excursion into other areas. The scale of the social scientist is therefore infinitesimally small compared with that of Professor Toynbee's book. His subjects are necessarily microcosmic. He does not intend to solve the problems of civilization and society by a frontal attack on the massed evidence of all the historical societies. All he hopes to do is so to organize the study of his minute topic as to be able to answer by the light of its evidence at least some of the problems which are common to society in general. In this he differs not only from the antiquarian, who is interested in his patch but has no questions to ask, but also from the philosophical historian, like Professor Toynbee, who has all the questions in the world to ask, but no patch on which even a single satisfactory answer can be raised.

There is no reason why Professor Toynbee should have written a work in sociology or social history. He has produced a great encyclopaedia, a brilliant anthology, and an essay in philosophic history. But until he writes a work of sociology he will not be able to rid himself of his vague images or to meet the challenge of his fruitful ones.

13

KARL MARX: A DEMOCRAT?[1]

I

It has been said of Marx's personality that it was a mixture of the humdrum and the heroic, heavily weighted on the side of the heroic. His life was a similar mixture, heavily weighted on the side of the humdrum. Much of what Marx did, and most of what was done to him, had its parallel in hundreds of other German lives in the first half of the nineteenth century; and the typical incidents, as distinguished from the exceptional ones, were evenly distributed over the whole of his life. He was born in 1818 in the town of Trier, into the family of a Jewish lawyer, and his early life and education were those of hundreds of other middle-class youths in Western Germany. On the material side there were the solid comforts of a society which had already recovered from the troubles of the Napoleonic wars and had not yet been thrown into the turmoil of the industrial revolution. Gymnasium and university followed as a matter of course; a professional and even a professorial career seemed to be predestined. On the cultural side there was the intellectual and artistic abundance of the 1830s. The period was one of transition, which, like many other periods of transition, enjoyed the best of both worlds; and it was on the best of both worlds that young Marx was reared.

From his father, a person of considerable culture, he obtained his knowledge of, and attachment to, the main tenets of eighteenth-century rationalism. A great friend of the family and his own father-in-law to be, Baron von Westphalen, introduced him to the new Romanticism. The resultant mixture equipped him well for the circle into which he fell in Berlin during the second year of his university studies. The intellectual fashions at the University of Berlin in the late thirties were dicatated by men who still considered themselves followers of the Hegelian tradition, but were in reality engaged in a revolt against the great idealist masters. The group of Hegelian left-wingers, led by men like Bruno Bauer, Ludwig Fauerbach and Karl Koppen, was trying to liberate the Hegelian logic, essentially one of flux and change, from subservience to philosophical and political conservatism. Into this group Marx fitted as a matter

[1] First published in *The Great Democrats*, ed. A. B. Brown (London, 1934).

of course. The mixed composition of his own youthful ideas enabled him to swallow easily Bruno Bauer's love-hatred of Hegelian philosophy, and it was under Bruno Bauer's influence and supervision that Marx pursued his somewhat irregular preparation for a learned career in Berlin and Jena.

If the promise of a learned career failed to materialize, the failure was due to forces outside Marx's own control and was shared by most of his friends. By 1840 political events succeeded in diverting the bulk of German youth from their intended vocations into a life of political struggle and adventure. The year 1841, when Marx was completing his doctorate thesis in Jena, witnessed the final extension of the official Prussian reaction to the universities, and with the reaction at its height there was as little chance of Marx entering the academic profession as there was of any of his friends remaining there. Bruno Bauer and most of his friends were chased out of universities and all had to take to journalism, politics and the life of professional *frondeurs*. And the life of journalism, politics and professional *fronde* had also to become the fate of young Marx. In 1841 he accepted a post on the *Rheinische Zeitung*, and his work on that left-wing paper was his first introduction to the life he was going to lead thereafter. As an introduction it was brief and highly ominous. In March 1842 Marx was forced to resign, and almost immediately afterwards the newspaper was suspended for what the Government considered its extreme opinions. With the end of the *Rheinische Zeitung* Marx, like most of his friends, emigrated abroad and, like most of his friends, took up his residence in Paris.

In Paris Marx moved yet another step further in the direction of political and social radicalism. It was there that he for the first time began to formulate the doctrines which eventually separated him from the rest of the young Hegelians and formed the basis of his future social and economic theory. It was above all in Paris that he became an avowed socialist. Even before his emigration he had shown some sympathy with the early manifestations of the French working-class movement. His residence in France enabled him to conceive for that movement something stronger and more definite than mere sympathy. Paris in the forties was all a–bubble with that political discontent and speculation out of which the new socialism was to rise. Disappointment in the false liberalism of Louis Philippe and his *haute bourgeoisie*, the intellectual exhaustion of eighteenth-century doctrines, the progress of the industrial revolution and the rise of the industrial proletariat – all these factors combined to produce in the France of the forties a veritable cataract of socialist activity. Into that cataract the bulk of the young German *émigrés*, and Marx among them, were drawn with irresistible power. His expulsion from France in 1845 and three years of residence in Brussels could do nothing to avert the progress of his socialist evolution. The publication of the *Heilige Familie*, written in collaboration with Engels, and the *Misère de la Philosophie* were important landmarks, leading directly to the Communist Manifesto, which he and Engels were to submit to the International Communist League in 1848. And it was in Paris that he met for the first time his life-long friend and collaborator, Friedrich Engels, now also moving towards a socialist point of view.

So when, in the spring of 1848, the revolution broke out in Germany and Marx was able to return to his native Rhineland, he arrived there as a fully-fledged socialist. Yet even now his destiny was not yet clear. It is difficult to say what exactly his life or his chances would have become had the democratic *régime* in Germany been established there and then, and had Marx been allowed to become one of its leaders. For while the revolutionary movement was still on the upgrade, he took up a very moderate attitude, refusing to join the separate communistic organizations and representing in the office of the *Neue Rheinische Zeitung*, which he was editing, the unity of the German radical left. But fates decreed that German democracy should not continue and that Marx should not become a republican statesman. In 1849 the Prussian reaction returned triumphant, and all the radical elements of German society – and Marx among them – had either to retire from journalism and politics or once more to emigrate abroad.

Thus we find Marx for the second time in exile, this time in London, concentrating on the preparation of the world's future, through sheer inability to affect Germany's present. From this time onwards his life ran its predestined course. From 1849 to 1855 there were the years of abject poverty in the slums of Soho, relieved by furious reading in the British Museum and work for the modest International (in reality, German) Communist League and the German Working-Men's Society in London. From 1855 to 1865 the material privations became less severe and the intellectual activity of the hunger years began to bear abundant fruit. The main outline of his economic and social doctrine took shape and the first International was finally established. And then from 1865 to 1875 there came the decade of fulfilment, with the first volume of *Das Kapital* out, the international movement strong and yet subservient to his views, all rivals in socialist theory and politics defeated and destroyed, he himself famous, feared and lionized. It was only after 1875 with the loss of his wife, ill-health and the demise of the International, that the constant progression of his life was arrested. Death came in 1883.

Thus all his life Marx travelled along a road which, however far it took him, always remained a highway, and never deteriorated into the solitary track of genius in the wilderness. Hundreds and thousands of other men and women, mostly young Germans, were travelling in the same direction, being converted to the same ideas and drawn into the ranks of the same movement. If Marx's life before 1846 followed the familiar pattern of a young German radical, his life after 1850 was shaped in the equally common mould of a cosmopolitan revolutionary and communist.

Yet Marx's was not an ordinary life. Into an existence which, for all its adventures, was often commonplace, he crowded a record of exceptional achievement – indeed so exceptional as to baffle all attempts at simple explanation. The lovers of the simple (and nearly all Marx's biographers fight shy of subtleties) find it easy to derive Marx's greatness from his intellectual genius. But the quantity and quality of his genius is very easy to exaggerate, for his intellectual greatness was largely relative to the mediocrity of his rivals and competitors. The only man in his *entourage* comparable with him in ability and knowledge was Engels, and Engels refused to compete. There is no denying that in his capacity for constructive generalization, in his logical powers, and in his intellectual vitality, Marx had few rivals in his generation, and that these qualities alone would have given him an exalted place among the sociological writers and political agitators of the mid-century. But he was more than a sociological writer or a political agitator: he was the prophet of a faith, and the leader of multitudes. And this he would never have become through his genius alone. There was a drive behind that machine which made it go further than its intellectual powers alone would have taken it. That drive came from the inner recesses of his character and will, and owed more to his emotions than to his intelligence. The lovers of the simple would perhaps describe it as 'ambition'. But however it is described and docketed, its origin need not be in doubt. Marx was a Jew, and a Jew in a community which had only just been emancipated from the medieval disabilities. Of this fact Marx always remained conscious, but it was not so much a conscious as an unconscious preoccupation with his racial origin that influenced his life. It was to this preoccupation that he probably owed his constant striving for the highest pinnacles of achievement. The first independent action of his life, his marriage to Jenny von Westphalen, had in it something of a daring aspiration. Jenny was older than Marx, very beautiful, rich, and, above all, very highly born, and his wooing and winning of Jenny was symbolical of the rest of his life. He attempted things which a man of less insatiable ambition would have shirked. He was not content just to write a book on political economy; he was going to produce a new science of economics. He would not merely improve upon the social philosophy of his predecessors; he was going to do for social philosophy what Darwin's *Origin of Species* did for biology. It was not his intention to lead a political party on behalf of a political reform; he was going to create an international movement that would shake the foundations of the world. Some of these designs were too vast to be achieved by any man, however great his genius. But they were sufficiently great to give a heroic scale to whatever Marx did achieve. He did not produce a new intellectual revolution, for his ideas were neither as new nor as revolutionary as he thought; but he came near enough to producing it to rank as one of the greatest social writers of all time. He did not shake the world as quickly and as profoundly as he hoped, but he came near enough to doing it to be considered as one of the greatest political leaders of the nineteenth century.

No doubt the combination of that peculiar genius with that extraordinary ambition had its shadowy side. The purely relative nature of Marx's genius was even more obvious to Marx himself than it is to us, and he was even more inclined to exaggerate the distance separating him from his fellow human beings than he had a right to do. His overwhelming and overweening conceit, his contempt for his adversaries, knew no bounds. They led him into innumerable, almost legendary, struggles against all other established leaders. His desperate battle with the German hot-heads in the fifties, his battle with Proudhon in 1867 and 1868, and with Bakunin from 1868 to 1872, filled his life with the continuous clash of arms; and if it is true that Marx's existence was one of unceasing struggle and war, the struggle was as much against adversaries as against adversities and the war was more against friends than against enemies.

Yet even the dark side of Marx's character was a help to achievement. But for his ruthless and unscrupulous handling of men, he might not have been able to impress his doctrines on his followers. Sometimes, indeed, he even impressed them on his enemies. There is nothing more moving in the history of communist leadership than the spectacle of Bakunin, after years of vicious and extremely painful attacks on his character by Marx and his friends, writing to Herzen to record his admiration for Marx's greatness and for his services to the socialist cause. There is more than a touch of pathos in the fact that in the later years of his life Bakunin was working on the Russian translation of *Das Kapital* and died with the work unfinished.

II

Marx's ideas were similarly a mixture of the generic and the individual, of things borrowed from the spirit of his age and things created anew. Least individual of all was his general philosophical outlook, and above all the scientific optimism and the evolutionary pre-suppositions inherent in his 'dialectical materialism'. Marx's materialism involved a belief that the laws of social life were as definite and as capable of being discovered as the laws of matter: a belief which he shared with all the scientific enthusiasts of his age. The characteristic mental state of advanced mid-Victorian thought was one of intellectual hope. Great as were the scientific achievements of the age, its scientific expectations were greater still. Men expected science not only to overcome the practical difficulties of existence, hunger and disease, but also to solve the accumulated multitude of intellectual problems, and to penetrate all the ancient mysteries of mankind and the universe. These expectations Marx shared to the full. In accordance with the spirit of the age he set out to discover the habits of society as a scientist discovers the habits of nature, to forecast and anticipate the action of social laws as a scientist forecasts and exploits the action of natural laws – in short, to create a new science of society, and thus to convert politics into a form of engineering, in which every action could be calculated, measured, foretold and controlled. Thus viewed, Marx's materialism was merely a variant of nineteenth-century 'positivism': a philosophical justification of his search for social laws.

It was not only in his search for social law in general but also in his predilection for a special kind of law that Marx proved himself to be a true son of his age. If the scientific preoccupation of the seventeenth and early eighteenth centuries was with physics, the greater scientific novelty of the nineteenth century was biology. Newton and Darwin each represented the most characteristic scientific achievement of their respective epochs. Just as the concept of the field of forces, thrust and counter-thrust, were the characteristic notions of the Newtonian age, so the evolutionary concepts, the laws of origin and transformation, were characteristic of the age of Darwin. The thought of that age, its politics and phraseology, were as full of evolution as ours is of relativity, and to this evolutionary mentality Marx paid a joyous tribute. The scientific laws which he tried to

159

lay bare were evolutionary laws; he sought to fit every situation that he was studying into an evolutionary curve: to enumerate the stages through which it passed, and to envisage its life-cycle as one of origin, maturity and decay. True, in common with most German evolutionary thinkers of the mid-nineteenth century, he tried to express his evolutionary notions in Hegelian phraseology, that is to say to represent the successive stages of evolution as parts of the Hegelian order of thesis, antithesis and synthesis. But, shorn of its cumbrous and barbaric phraseology, this Hegelian logic, as employed by Marx, merely expressed the evolutionary nature of the social process. All it meant was that every stage of development rested on the preceding stage and itself formed the starting-point for any stage to come. It is, therefore, no wonder that Marx regarded himself as the Darwin-in-chief of sociology and his own 'dialectical materialism' as an evolu-tionary re-interpretation of social life.

From this philosophical position, typical of his age and common to most of his contemporaries, Marx proceeded by steps of his own towards the social theory and political programme that bear his name. The link was provided, not by his much discussed and now exploded 'labour theory of value', but by his 'economic interpretation of history'. In spite of the enormous amount of space given to the theory of value in *Das Kapital* it was in reality outside his main body of doctrine and unnecessary for the logical sequence of his ideas. The economic intepretation of history, on the other hand, followed most naturally from his general outlook. To a materialist in search of a materialist interpretation of society, economic phenomena offer an obvious opening. There is nothing easier than to assume that what matter is to animal life and the physical world, economic realities are to society and culture. They are concerned with elementary facts of human existence and thus also with the most essential conditions of social life. It was therefore in full consonance with the accepted materialist attitude that Marx made his famous distinction between the economic basis of society and its 'ideological superstructure': the organiza-tion of production and distribution on the one hand and legal institutions, religious beliefs and philosophical ideas on the other. Of course Marx was too much of a philosopher and too much of an historian ever to have alleged, as he is sometimes accused of doing, that non-economic pheno-mena had no effect on the course of history. In most of his historical examples he was careful to show how the political facts and ideas affected those very economic relations from which they were derived. But that they did derive he never doubted. Behind the complexity of historical events he always saw the great economic cause, the one source from which everything else sprang and to which everything else could be reduced and related.

This original economic source Marx sometimes described in its simplest and crudest form. Every element of society and culture and every important movement in history could directly be explained by the material needs of men and their instruments of production. But on the whole, this cruder and simpler version of economic materialism is more typical of *epigoni*, of the followers and vulgarizers of the Marxian theory, than of Marx himself. He himself, oftener than not, used the word 'economic' in a sense far subtler than that implied in the vulgar versions of economic determinism. The economic factor determining history and society is something more than the animal urges of hunger, thirst and lust, or the inanimate matter employed in their satisfaction. What Marx had in mind is the economic activity of society, the way society organizes its production and distribution. In the process of production and distribution different economic functions are assigned to different groups of producers; their shares of the profits are apportioned and their mutual relations ordered. It is through the 'social relations of production' that economic factors shape history and culture. And it is the social relations of production that are implied in the term 'economic' in Marx's own version of economic materialism.

This concept of social relations of production links Marx's sociology to what is probably the most important of his generalizations, that of class and class war. Social relations of production are essentially relations between classes. Marx assumed that men performing the same economic functions and thus occupying the same economic positions in the productive system fall into natural groups or, as he called them, social classes. And as every new system of production rearranges and redistributes the economic functions of men, it also creates a class structure of its own. The economic system of medieval agricultural production was characterized by a feudal structure of society; the emergence of capitalism was accompanied by the appearance of a modern class structure, the *bourgeoisie* and the proletariat. In the process of historical transformation the ruling classes of old disappear, new ruling classes emerge, the orders of superiority and inferiority, subordination and superordination, change and reverse. A state of constant class war is therefore inevitable, for rising classes must fight their way to domination, ruling classes must fight to maintain their positions. And in that war legal institutions and constitutional forms are but weapons, political and legal changes are but battles won and lost.

With this final twist, with the substitution of class war for social relations of production and for production itself, the Marxian theory of
history merges into his political programme. It offers immense opportunities for political application, and in these opportunities its real
originality is to be found. By explaining the social mechanism of historical
change Marx was able to envisage the mechanism of the changes to come,
or, to be more exact, to construct the mechanism of the changes to be
brought about. What Marx himself endeavoured to bring about was the
establishment of a socialist order in the interests of the working classes,
and to this endeavour the class theory of history offered a certain hope and
a direct indication for action. To present history as an endless record of
the rise and fall of classes, was to raise hopes before the subject classes
of the age. But what converted the hope into a certainty was Marx's
insistence on the youth of the proletariat and on its connection with the
modern industrial system. Doctored up in the Hegelian way this insistence became a prophecy. It revealed the proletariat as that new power
which, in accordance with the 'dialectics of the historical process', was
maturing in the womb of the very system it was destined to destroy. In
other words, the economic interpretation of history, and with it the rest of
Marxian philosophy, became a way of assuring the working classes that
they were bound to win.

Even more important from a political point of view was the immediate
bearing which this version of economic materialism had on the problem
of socialist tactics. If all fundamental historical change is wrought by
class war and if the transition to socialism necessarily involves a struggle
between capitalists and the proletariat, then socialism can be achieved
only by a proletarian victory in the capitalist class war. The attempts of the
earlier socialists to achieve a socialist society by the immediate and piece-
meal establishment of socialist communities or workshops within the
present social system were, from Marx's point of view, utopian and
dangerous. Under capitalist conditions they could not survive, and
they could not affect the social system even if they did. What is more,
they diverted the working classes from the concentration on class war,
which should be the chief object of a truly socialist movement.

In this way the Marxian social and political theory became a justification
for the objects and strategy of the socialist organization which Marx was
directing. Of course it would be unjust to Marx to regard his theories as
a mere adjunct to a political programme. Shorn of its political implications
the Marxian philosophy still remains a doctrine of great intellectual and
scientific force, capable of holding its own by the sheer breadth of its

generalizations and the power of its logic. Yet it is not its scientific generalizations or its logic that have given it its unique place in the history of modern times. On intellectual and scientific grounds alone it would hardly have outshone or outlived, as it certainly has done, the multitude of political and sociological theories of the mid-nineteenth century. If Marx is still a leading force today, while men like Comte and Spencer are mere fodder for the sociologist, it is because he did not confine himself to science and philosophy, while Comte and Spencer did. He hitched his science to a star, and it was his great fortune that the star was Aurora herself, the morning star of the rising political faith.

III

The political implications of Marxian philosophy, however, are too inconsistent to give him a secure seat among the nineteenth-century democrats. Democracy as a political creed benefited relatively little and suffered a great deal from Marx and his followers. Yet there is one sense of the word 'democracy' and one aspect of Marx's activity which entitle him to a place in the gallery of great democrats. Democracy may mean several things. It may mean the belief in certain forms of government: government by the majority, representative institutions. It may also mean a certain conception of the functions and power of the state: government by consent and aversion from compulsion and force. Neither of these two variants of democracy derives much support from Marx's writings and activity. Belief in the absolute value of representative government is inconsistent with the view of all constitutional forms as a mere expression of class power, while belief in government by consent is inconsistent with the view of historical progress as a product of class war. It is, therefore, no wonder that Marxian theory has so commonly been used as an armoury of arguments against the political tenets of liberal democracy. Much of the cynical attitude of modern communists towards parliament and elected majorities and much of the argument in favour of proletarian dictatorship derives naturally and easily from Marx's writings.

Yet it would be wrong to respect Marxian thought as anti-democratic. Useful as it may have been to the advocates of communist dictatorship of our own age, it has many affinities with the liberal and democratic faith of the age of Marx. For democracy can have yet another meaning, more general and in a sense more fundamental than either the belief in representative institutions or the dislike of government by force. Democracy is not only a theory of government, but also a scale of moral values.

As a scale of values it belongs to the European tradition of humanitarian individualism. It accepts human personality and individual man as an end in themselves, the sole purpose and the only justification of a social system. It judges political actions by the good or evil they do to individuals, rather than by their effects on the collective super-individual entities of race, state, church and society. Between this view of life and the political programme of democracy there is a natural connection. Majority rule, representative institutions, government by consent and respect for opinions are merely broad applications of humanitarian ethics to problems of state government. Nevertheless, the link, natural as it is, need not always be accepted. It does not require more than the usual allowance of inconsistency to believe in the ethical principle of democracy without subscribing to its political applications, or to accept its political forms without believing in the underlying ethical principle.

This is exactly what Marx did. His allowance of inconsistency was if anything above the average: and it not infrequently enabled him to travel far and fortunately beyond the logical confines of his theory. Sceptical as he was of the absolute virtue of democratic forms and prone as he was to take a realist view of government, he yet betrayed over and over again his unquestioning and almost instinctive dependence on the ethical principle of modern democracy. This principle he owed to his father and to his father's friends, to the whole of the enlightened humanitarian influences to which he was exposed in his childhood. He shared it throughout his life with his friends of the Prussian left, the neo-Hegelians, the liberals, radicals, and socialists, and he handed it over to the first generation of German social-democrats. It was deeply embedded in the whole of the social thought of the time and was taken for granted to an extent which made its public and conscious avowal by Marx as unnecessary as it was difficult.

It was this liberal and humanitarian predisposition which threw him in his early student days into the company of the philosophical radicals in Berlin, which led him at the very beginning of his adult life into opposition to the reactionary government of Prussia, and which assisted in his conversion to socialism. We know from his articles and correspondence that what for the first time attracted his attention to socialism was the pity and the pathos of the unsuccessful working-class movements in the forties. If in the course of the subsequent years he moved a great deal further in the direction of socialism, he was led as much by a fervid compassion for down-trodden humanity as by intellectual conviction. The fervour may have been prophetic and Hebraic in its origin; but the pity and compassion were wholly German, sentimental and nineteenth-century, something alien to the callous century that preceded it and almost equally alien to the century which followed.

Nowhere, however, does the liberal inspiration of Marxian ideas emerge more fully than in his conception of the future socialist order. Unlike the utopian socialists, Marx was very careful not to construct imaginary schemes of the socialist state. In his abumbration of the socialist society he confined himself to a few vague ideals. But vague and general as these may have been, they were ideals. They represented Marx's standard of values: his final measure of good and evil. It is therefore doubly significant to find that the Marxian image of the socialist paradise embodies the essentials of a liberal and democratic order. The transition from capitalism to socialism will be the transition from the kingdom of necessity to the kingdom of freedom. The kingdom of freedom will be that state of classless co-operation, social harmony and fulfilment of individual personality, which simple liberals hope to achieve within the confines of the present economic system. In other words, where Marx differed from the common run of liberals was not in his conception of the democratic ideal, but in its timing. If Marx denied the democratic programme, his denials were all qualified by an implied 'for the time being'. From the point of view of his final objects, democracy was not only consistent with socialism, but was its purpose and justification.

Nevertheless, had this democratic faith been confined to the realms of final objects, had it remained mere *Zukunftsmusik*, critics would still have been justified in regarding Marx's message as unrelated, if not inimical, to the democratic movement in the modern world. Marx's democratic outlook, however, revealed itself in ways more definite and more immediate. It influenced some of his political utterances and decisions in direct opposition to the dictatorial and anti-democratic tendency in others. We know that Marx's chief contribution to modern socialist tactics was his advocacy of the participation of the proletariat in the politics of the modern state. To him the struggle for unrestricted franchise, and the exercise of political power which that franchise offered, was the most urgent part of socialist action. True, he usually represented this political activity as a mere extension of class war and the preparation for the socialist revolution; but on more than one occasion he emphasized the fact that the political emancipation of the working classes was to be desired for its own sake.

It is this happy inconsistency in Marx's attitude to the democratic politics of the day that gives special significance to his struggle against the revolutionary adventurers in the socialist movement. The struggle began in earnest in 1847 when Marx was opposed by Weitling, a German working-man conspirator, and continued in 1848 when Marx thwarted an insane project of Herwegh (a revolutionary poet who put more poetry into his revolution than into his poems) to invade Prussia at the head of a legion of German revolutionaries. It was resumed in 1850 during the conflict with the party of direct action in the International Communist League. It was taken up again in the successive clashes with Mazzini, the French anarchist Proudhon, and above all, the Russian anarchist Bakunin. In all these recurrent struggles Marx was doubtless led by a whole medley of motives. There was, in the first place, the natural caution of a shrewd observer, sceptical of the outcome of the revolutionary attempts and anxious to save the young communist movement from inevitable failures. There was also a motive which can, with a certain amount of circumlocution, be described as a personal dislike of physical adventure not untinged with emotional aversion from danger. There was, above all, the insistence on the inexorable march of economic events and on the futility of political action in advance of economic evolution. But in addition to all these motives there was a definite opposition to the political outlook of the revolutionary wholesalers. He was often prepared to assume that 'to-morrow will be finer than today', and that the gifts tomorrow may bring must not be spurned. This assumption stood in curious contrast to his economic theory of the growing insecurity of capitalism and the impoverishment of the working classes. In some moods he would argue that that very impoverishment would facilitate the coming of a socialist revolution, but in others he seemed to think that the progress of which capitalism was capable was facilitating, if not the establishment of a socialist order, at any rate a greater measure of political and social action by the working classes.

When in this mood Marx invariably found himself adhering to the liberal and democratic opinion of his day. Some of that adherence was unconscious and unintentional; some of it definitely was not. On more than one occasion Marx openly allied himself with the other progressive forces. There was not a single liberal cause in the sixties and seventies which he did not make his own. He was an enthusiastic and steadfast admirer of Lincoln. Remote as his own class doctrine was from Lincoln's grandiloquent idealism, and difficult as he found it to represent the Yankee war against the South as an incident in the proletarian struggle, he never-theless remained to the last a supporter of the great president. He was caught in the wave of humanitarian sentiment raised by the anti-slavery issue, and on the crest of that wave he remained until the end of Lincoln's days. To realize what this attitude meant it is enough to compare it with the attitude of a modern communist to Franklin Roosevelt, or to any other leader of the liberal and democratic movements of our own day. And what is true of his attitude to Lincoln is true of his attitude to the other liberal causes of his time. Thus his interest in the Irish movement was unflagging. Though he sometimes tried to dress up his pro-Irish attitude in the phraseology of the Communist Manifesto, no ingenuity, not even his own, could represent the possible triumph of the nationalists in Ireland as a contribution to the proletarian class war. What in reality commended that movement to Marx was its liberal aura, its struggle for freedom and its connection with the humanitarian issues to which every democrat in Europe responded as a matter of course. And what is true of his attitude to Ireland is also true of his attitude to the liberal movements in Italy and Hungary and Russia. He disliked Gladstone as a personification of middle-class hypocrisy and a sanctimonius humbug, yet the party which was to become Gladstone's, the liberals and radicals of England, often received from Marx a measure of support as unexpected as it was unsolicited.

It goes without saying that these excursions into democratic camps could be matched by similar excursions in the opposite direction. We know that towards the end of his life Marx was engaged in a desperate fight to prevent the adoption by the German social-democratic party of the so-called Gotha programme in which parliamentary and democratic politics were regarded as almost equal to the socialist purposes of the party. In the course of this fight Marx gave expression to points of view which were far nearer to the pure substance of his original class theory than most of his other political declarations and which have been used since to great effect by modern communists and anti-democratic socialists. The nature of that attack can very easily be misunderstood, for, like most of Marx's other charges, it was directed against more than one objective. A wounded sense of proprietorship must have played an important part. The movement which he had nurtured to life, and which he had come to regard as his own, suddenly began to frame its policies for itself and to disregard its maker's orders. But there is no doubt at all that Marx found himself alarmed by the political possibilities of the programme. He feared that the striving for immediate political and social reforms, which the Gotha programme sanctioned, might lead the movement away from its final objectives. The fear arose naturally from Marx's social philosophy, and was nearer to the letter of his doctrine than were his democratic

policies. Judged by the letter of his doctrine Marx's humanitarian pre-
suppositions and liberal sympathies were mere inconsistencies. But then
in his attitude to the state, as in his character and life, there was a great
deal of inconsistency. It is owing to his inconsistency, as much as to his
greatness, that we can rank him among the democrats of the nineteenth
century, and indeed among that century's truest sons.

14

HUGH GAITSKELL: POLITICAL AND INTELLECTUAL PROGRESS[1]

The fifteen or sixteen years between 1930 and 1945 saw important changes in Hugh Gaitskell's personal circumstances: his coming to London, his academic post at University College, his involvement with party work, his earliest election campaign, his year of study and socialist rising in Vienna, his entry into Government service with the outbreak of war, his friendship and collaboration with Hugh Dalton, and, overlaying all this, his marriage. I propose to confine myself to what I know of his political and intellectual progress in this period. We were close friends, constantly in each other's company, more especially in the years between 1929 and 1934 when I lived in London, and again between 1939 and 1943 when we both worked in the Ministry of Economic Warfare and lived in Eileen Power's and my house in Mecklenburgh Square. Moreover, our friendship was exceedingly socratic and even didactic. We argued incessantly and incontinently all the time we were together, even on walking holidays in the Lakes or at dancing parties at the Gargoyle. As a result we came to know or to believe we knew one another's ideas almost as well as our own.

I knew Hugh Gaitskell slightly in his Nottingham years. We had met once in a WEA class on the Industrial Revolution, which he was conducting, and again a few months later during his visit to London at a party given by John Gray, then a young sociologist at LSE. Such, however, was my lack of perception that I did not carry away a clear or a true impression of Hugh as a person. In Nottingham he struck me as one of the typical Oxbridge left-wingers who were a drug on the market in those days. At a London party we conversed for a while, but to me he appeared merely as another of the well-spoken Bloomsburyites of the second generation – Nineteen-Seventeen-Club, Cave of Harmony and all that.

I came to realize how mistaken I was a year later when circumstances brought us closely together. We were both junior lecturers at University College, and towards the end of the first term of 1930 we found ourselves

---

[1] First published in *Hugh Gaitskell*, ed. W. T. Rodgers (London, 1964).

sitting opposite each other at the annual dinner of the Professional Dining Club. The occasion was very convivial and wine was both good and plentiful; so when we found ourselves alone he turned to me with a question much more direct than one he would have allowed himself on a more sober occasion. 'I see you are not a fool, but I am told you hold *émigré* views about Russia: how can you?' And thus started the first of the many, indeed hundreds, of dialogues between us on politics, social philosophy, socialism, Russia, economics, methodology. In this very first dialogue Hugh already was fully the man he was to show himself in intimate debate throughout the years that followed: an ideal listener, attentive and courteous, full of respect for his collocutor and anxious to meet him most of the way, yet too concerned in the subject matter and too firm in his own views ever to pretend to agree for mere politeness or to retreat beyond the main line of his defence.

Within less than a year of this first encounter Evan Durbin, an Oxford friend of Hugh's and another recent recruit to University College, joined us in the conversations. By 1930 they had already arrived at a mutual understanding which for newcomers like myself was, to begin with almost impenetrable. They were, of course, too different as persons to agree on every subject. Evan Durbin was already set in his views, which were essentially those he was to hold for the rest of his life, whereas Hugh Gaitskell was still very much on the move. The touch of finality in Durbin's convictions was of immense value to Hugh who came to rely upon the assured, down-to-earth, good sense which Evan appeared to ooze out of every pore. Hugh would often take from Evan propositions which he might decline when offered by others, and it often fell to Evan to act as a broker between Hugh and his other friends.

Our triangle was by no means self-sufficient. Hugh's ideas and interests in psychology (in common with most of his contemporaries he was for a time a convinced Freudian) were served by another friend of Evan Durbin's, John Bowlby. On rare but immensely important occasions we had R. H. Tawney with us. He had got to know Hugh and Evan through Eileen Power and myself, and developed a great liking for them. But needless to say our encounters with Tawney never took the form of ordinary discussions. In his company we were prepared to sit and listen, amused by the wit and aptness of his language and enraptured by the image of the man himself, to us the greatest living Englishman. The views he held happened to be very near those to which Hugh was moving by himself, but from Tawney's conversation they always emerged washed clean of all triviality and glowing with his philosophy and poetry.

Hugh Gaitskell

From 1931 onwards, more especially in the war years when Hugh came to live with us, most of our encounters and discussions took place in Eileen Power's presence, usually at our house in Mecklenburgh Square. I believe it was she who brought Gaitskell and Durbin to Dalton's notice. I was present at the dinner party in 1930 to which Dalton and Tawney were invited by Eileen to meet them; and I remember having to defend ourselves, after Hugh and Evan had gone, against Dalton's accusation of 'hoarding' for our exclusive use these 'charming young socialists'.

Some of our discussions took place in gatherings which were relatively large and formally constituted. One such series of gatherings was organized by Hugh and Evan in 1931 to discuss the economics of socialist society. The early meetings of the group were in the basement of Bogey's Bar, a café which John Bowlby and Durbin ran for several years in the building of the Royal Hotel. The first meeting was heavily weighted by young economists of whom James Meade was one; surprisingly enough Roy Harrod also attended on one or two occasions. As the thirties advanced, the meetings were transferred to the London School of Economics and became somewhat less formal.

These meetings petered out in the early years of the war, but one of these war-time gatherings which may or may not have been a part of the series stands out very clearly in my memory. It was a largely informal encounter in my flat in 1943 with George Woodcock, now Secretary of the TUC. What we discussed was the place of the professional *élite* in social movements. Woodcock remained highly sceptical and poured scorn on the evanescent socialism of young middle-class intellectuals. This resistance of Woodcock's apparently greatly impressed Hugh, who confided to me on the following day his fear that it would take a long time to wean English socialists away from the traditional identification of socialism with the industrial proletariat. 'They will be shocked, and they will call us fascists.'

Wholly different, more academic in purpose and composition, was the group which Eileen Power and others, with Hugh's encouragement, formed in 1932 to discuss the sociological and historical implications of economic problems. The list of papers presented to the group which I still possess contains the names, in addition to our own, of Walter Adams (now Vice-Chancellor in the University of Southern Rhodesia), T. H. Marshall, D. W. Brogan, and John Hawgood (now Professor of History in Birmingham).

More infrequent but nevertheless quite significant for Hugh's political development were our attendances at *Tots and Quots*. This was a dining club formed by G. P. (Gip) Wells and Solly Zuckerman, which met on Saturday nights in *Quo Vadis*, a Soho restaurant, to discuss scientific method. I always suspected that the original inspiration behind the dinners was Gip Wells's liking for good food in congenial company, but the official purpose was to expound the unity of scientific method in all fields of inquiry, political and economic as well as purely scientific. In those days the phrase 'unity of scientific method' had a distinct Marxist ring. The intention of the founders was to assemble men of many specialities and of every shade of opinion (*tot homines, quot opiniones*), but the attendance and the ideas were largely provided by the Marxist or near-Marxist scientists. 'Sage' Bernal was frequently there and was as always forceful and prolific. I came very infrequently and read a paper only once, but Hugh came more often, partly for the sake of the wine and the food, but mainly because he was at that time passing through a phase in which Marxists and their talk drew him irresistibly by the very provocation they caused. Such anti-Marxist predispositions as he already had were strengthened by what he heard and discussed at *Quo Vadis*.

These various groups and encounters formed the background to Hugh's intellectual life in the thirties or rather to that side of his life which I observed. It goes without saying that his universe was much wider. He was after all a serious, indeed a dedicated, economist, and was also increasingly drawn into the political and administrative activities of the Labour Party. He knew well all the economists at LSE (for a time in Oxford he had been Lionel Robbins's pupil), and was very friendly with both N. Kaldor and Thomas Balogh. However, the economist with whom he was most intimate was his colleague at University College, Paul Rosenstein Rodan, a man of immense erudition, ingenuity, and generosity, who greatly contributed to Hugh's development as an economist.

Finally, there were the miscellaneous friendships which Hugh formed so easily and maintained so firmly. Some dated from his Winchester and Oxford days and even his days at the Dragon School. Among these friendships which were to mature and deepen in London was that with Frank Pakenham, who at one time shared rooms with him in Oxford, and with his wife Elizabeth. Different again was another Oxford friendship which Hugh shared with Evan – that of John MacMurray, who inspired them in Oxford as a teacher of philosophy but who soon became a colleague and a close friend at UCL. Hugh also spoke of Maurice Bowra as one of his most rewarding Oxford friendships, and of John Betjeman, whom he had known at the Dragon and in Oxford.

His Bloomsbury contacts also ripened into a large number of friendships which I cannot enumerate here. Two of these friendships I must, however, single out – that with the Mitchisons and that with Amyas Ross. For a period in 1932 the Mitchison household in Hammersmith provided him with a stimulating and varied company of left-wing intellectuals, and for this and other reasons was for a time something of a magnet. On the other hand Amyas Ross, a gentle and feckless waif, one of Bloomsbury's earliest beatniks, was a source of constant preoccupation. Hugh, together with another friend, founded the Soho Gallery, sellers and publishers of modern reproductions, mainly in order to provide Ross with an occupation. In the war Hugh got Dalton to give Ross employment in the Ministry of Economic Warfare and even persuaded Ross to put on a dark suit and to keep office hours. Those who know Hugh can easily imagine his distress when a few months later Ross was found dead in his sordid little apartment off New Oxford Street – dead from neglect after 'flu. Overshadowing all these personal contacts and friendships were his emotional links with his elder brother Arthur, whose infrequent visits to London on leave from Sudan were times of great upheaval; and of course his link with his wife. Few people know and only Hugh himself could have recounted all that Dora meant and did for him in those years – the care she lavished on him when he needed it most, the understanding and stimulus he found in her company. And Hugh alone knew how much he owed to her advice and to her steady and persistent influence.

At the time of our earliest discussions – in 1929 and 1930 – Hugh Gaitskell's socialist convictions appeared at first sight to be of the typical inter-war Oxbridge variety. They were couched in language which was nothing if not radical. The word 'class war', 'social revolution', and 'proletariat' rolled off his tongue easily and smoothly, and the words 'intellectual' and 'middle-class' he used as often as not as terms of opprobrium. He was perhaps already too much of an economist to speak glibly of capitalist exploitation and wage slavery, but the memories of the General Strike and the coal strike and his personal experiences of working-class life in Nottinghamshire had bitten deeply into him. He thought of poverty, inequality, unemployment and slums with emotion and spoke of them with heat. I do not remember his using in private discussion the formula of 'common ownership of the means of production', but I do not think it occurred to him at that time to question nationalization of industry as the crowning object of socialism. In spite of all his doubts about the Soviet Union he still spoke of it as 'the great socialist country' and blamed the faults of the Soviet régime on the Russian national character.

To us in the earliest thirties all this was familiar stuff: the typical assortment of ideas most young socialists held at the time. Yet what struck me at our very first conversation at the Professorial Dinner Club was the note of doubt he sounded every time he brought out a stock idea. This condition of incipient heterodoxy may have come from having been previously treated to G. D. H. Cole's unorthodox variants of socialism. But in Hugh's case many of the doubts were of too recent an origin to be traceable to Cole. They bore the mark of 1930, and they grew from year to year in the subsequent decade.

Contrary to the 'rightist' image which Hugh acquired in later years, the one aspect of Hugh's socialism which appeared to me to change least in the thirties and early forties was its radicalism. Until 1945 (and our contacts after that date became too infrequent for me to be able to judge) Hugh preserved almost intact his emotional predilection for radical solutions. Again, contrary to his public image of later years he was by temperament, or rather by logic, a whole-hogger. This showed itself in his policy in MEW on blockade and neutral rights; in the influence he had on the 1949 devaluation, more drastic than that favoured by many of his colleagues; in the manner in which he chose to present his opposition to Clause 4, and in his final attitude to the Common Market. On all these occasions he was of course concerned with immediate political issues, not with final socialist objectives, but those who knew him best would probably agree that both before and after 1945 the vision of equality which inspired his socialism was more intense and more far-reaching than that of most Labour politicians. Where he changed most in the thirties was not so much in the intensity of his views as in their contents, i.e. not in their quantity but in their essence: in the intellectual make-up of his socialist ideal.

To my mind (the scale of priorities is entirely my own) the most fundamental of these changes was his gradual abandonment of the proletarian sociology of socialism. In the end, i.e. by 1945, his views on class demarcations and on the alignment of interests for and against socialism came to resemble the views which historians of socialism would recognize as 'populist'. When we first met he was writing, or had just finished writing, an essay on the Chartists, and the question which bothered him most was the social make-up of the Chartist movement. How was it, he asked, that the advocates of revolutionary action and the early socialists found their following not so much among the rising class of industrial proletariat as among the *déclassé* victims of the Industrial Revolution, mainly refugees from petit-bourgeois occupations?

These doubts prepared the ground for the continued discussions of this problem in the following decade. In 1931 and 1932 I devoted a large part of my course on the economic history of great powers at LSE to the recent trends in the social structure of industrial employment and above all to the proliferation of the various *élites* and the relative decline in the semi-skilled employments. Evan Durbin who attended the course suggested that we might try to work out the implications of this trend for socialist policy. These implications had already come up in earlier discussions with Hugh and Evan, and it is therefore not surprising that they should have occupied us at a number of the earliest meetings in Bogey's Bar. In the end Durbin incorporated his and our ideas on this subject into his *Politics of Democratic Socialism*. On his part Hugh gradually made up his mind that the whole conception of socialism would have to be fitted to a future wherein the personnel of industry and the political following of popular parties would be composed of those very elements whom the *Communist Manifesto* dismissed as the fellow-travellers of the bourgeoisie. This topic preoccupied Hugh during a memorable week-end he spent in Cambridge in 1936, and this was also the topic which he repeatedly brought up at the gatherings of Eileen Power's sociological group. If on my return to London in 1939 the subject no longer entered into our conversation with any frequency, this was mainly because Durbin's book was already completed and Hugh's views on the subject appeared to be fully formed. Woodcock's reaction to our somewhat extreme exposition of the idea disturbed Hugh, precisely because it boded ill for future chances of transmuting the social appeal of socialism.

Hugh's views on the sociology of socialism developed concurrently with his views of nationalization. I do not know how far the ethos of Cole's 'guild socialism' or of Tawney's *Acquisitive Society* were responsible for his earliest doubts about nationalization as the only way of conducting industry in a socialist society. Evan, in his empirical fashion, insisted on discussing the virtues and vices of nationalization not as an ideal and not in global terms but pragmatically, industry by industry. This we frequently did at the meetings at Bogey's Bar. On my own part I pressed on Hugh my conviction that all-embracing state ownership, as in Soviet Russia, was compatible with a society more inimical to the real purposes of socialism than even Baldwin's England. In addition Hugh and Evan were drawn into the debate on socialist planning and pricing systems which proceeded all through the thirties among the younger

Fact and relevance

LSE economists and in which for a time Abraham Lerner and Paul Sweezy (both at that time near-communists) were most active. From this debate we all emerged with the conviction that the economic purposes of socialism could be attained by properly inspired and properly conducted central planning, and that for a socialist transformation of the economy the 'command of the strategic heights' (a typical pre-war formula!) would suffice.

My impression, however, is that all these influences provided the make-weight, not the mainspring, of Hugh's evolution. He was moving and would have moved in this direction by his own momentum. For to him the essence of socialism always was equality and social justice; and, as far as I can remember, he always declared himself to be uncommitted to the choice of means. When he came to consider practical proposals for individual industries or for land he invariably turned out to be more radical than Evan or some of his other friends. I also know from some of our infrequent discussions in the late fifties that, had he been then in power, his shopping list of industries and interests to be nationalized would have been far wider than that of many of the defenders of Clause 4. He was not, however, prepared to identify socialism with nationalization of industry; and to this view he had come to be firmly wedded by 1939 at the very latest.

These views of socialist purposes, class alignments and common ownership were of course highly un-Marxist. When I first met him his conversation was still larded with Marxian phraseology and he still found amusement in jokes about my 'anti-Marxist prejudice'. Like all economists of that time, he rejected the labour theory of value and dismissed as beside the point the whole Marxist economic theory, including his theory of crises (Joan Robinson's preoccupations with vols. II and III of *Das Kapital* came more than a decade later). But while rejecting Marxian economics he took it for granted that Marxian sociology and economic history still held good and were proper intellectual tools for a socialist to employ.

Yet even at that time his Marxian attachments were very fragile. I have already mentioned his early doubts about Marxist class analysis, and I soon discovered that his general outlook was not materialist and certainly not dialectical. Dialectics were to him the most unpalatable ingredient of Marxian philosophy. The dialectical jargon current among his contemporaries – the 'negation of the negation', 'the transmutation of quantity into quality' and all the rest of it – were wholly alien to his mode of speaking and thinking. One night in 1934 on our walk through Soho after

a long session with a certain communist mathematician, Hugh proclaimed –
somewhat angrily as if the fault were mine – that he found the whole
system of dialectical notions hollow and boring. To please me he had
struggled through the *Anti-Dühring* and blamed me for it ever after. In
fact in spite of my anti-Marxist views I often found myself acting as an
advocatus diaboli trying to commend to Hugh the subtleties of Marxian
exegesis. But in general he preferred to hear the ideology expounded and
defended by those who believed in it. This may have been one of the
uses to which he put his encounters with the Marxists at the *Tots and
Quots*.

On another nocturnal walk home after a meeting which discussed a paper
on class conflicts he inveighed against the self-contained logic of the dialectic. When I replied that it was no more self-contained than the logic
of marginal economics or of Freudian psychology, he came back with
strictures on the individual propositions of Marxian ideology and especially
on the proposition that evolution proceeded by conflicts of opposites,
or that significant class demarcations were always determined by social
relations of production, or that the economic factor was at the base of
social phenomena, or that there was a meaningful distinction between
'base' and 'superstructure'. In his frequent conversational inquests on
the Austro-German social democrats he invariably spoke of their Marxism
as one of their afflictions.

This, I believe, became his settled opinion some time before the war.
In 1935 I sent him from Cambridge a reprint of an essay on Marx, which
I had contributed to Barrett Brown's *Great Democrats*, and he wrote back
to say that the whole world of Marxist ideas was now so remote from his real
preoccupations that he had lost all interest in it and that it was about
time I did likewise.

His views on Russia were not influenced by his revulsion from Marxism,
but they nevertheless moved in the same direction. His youthful notions
about Russia as a great socialistic experiment and about the temporary and
self-healing character of the Soviet dictatorship did not survive for very
long. My own stories and views may have contributed to his disillusion-
ments, and so did also his contacts with continental social democrats.
He read widely into the current literature about the USSR, but distrusted
much of what he read and strongly reacted against the tales brought back
by the returning hordes of 'intourists'. On the other hand he met through
me a number of Western experts who had served the Soviet régime or
spent some time in Russia on specialist assignments. The report which I
believe had the greatest effect on him was that of the well-known Canadian

agricultural adviser, Cairns, who had made an extended study of Stalin's collectivization and whom we saw a great deal on his way back from Russia. Stalin's régime with its accumulation of lies and horrors had of course the same effect on Hugh as it had on other socialists in the 1930s; and when the war broke out his position in the intelligence branch of MEW enabled him to see a great deal of information which confirmed his worst views of Stalin's régime. He had been among the very few of my friends who were neither surprised nor unduly shocked by the Molotov–Ribbentrop agreement.

Yet it is curious how inconspicuous Hugh Gaitskell's attitude to Russia remained. During the war the Russian section of MEW was one of my responsibilities, and we in the Ministry not only formed an optimistic view of Russia's capacity to withstand the German invasion, but also took the initiative in organizing the economic assistance to Russia. The Ministry therefore acquired in some Government circles the reputation of being specially pro-Russian, and of reflecting thereby the socialist sympathies of Dalton and Gaitskell. Only Hugh's friends knew how far apart even at that time were Hugh's sympathies from his judgment of political and military necessities.

His attitudes to the Soviet régime and still more his attitude to Nazi Germany reflected not only his political views but also his own brand of Englishry. He was deeply English in most things, including his political attitudes; and by degrees these attitudes became sufficiently conscious to become a subject of debate between him, Evan Durbin and myself. Needless to say, Hugh's nationalism was entirely a matter of loyalties and allegiances and was utterly devoid of any phobias. He had numerous foreign friends and easily associated with foreigners in England and abroad. In recent years several prominent socialists abroad confessed to me that they found him the most congenial of the English Labour leaders. These sympathies went together with his liking for foreign travel. In this respect he was very unlike Durbin who was never happy away from England and preferred the Cotswolds and Cornwall to all other holiday playgrounds. Yet although Gaitskell used to chide Durbin for his insularity, he invariably placed his own socialist ideas and his visions of the future in a purely English setting. In one of our conversations with Tawney in 1933 we got Tawney to describe his work in the slums of pre-1914 Manchester, and heard him say that all through that time he felt humiliated by the sight of 'his fellow Englishmen' in their abject condition. Later, when left alone with Hugh, I commented on the words used – fellow Englishmen, not fellow human beings – but Hugh, after a brief pause, confessed that he would have used the same words. He had reasoned himself into international socialism, but his vision of the future was one of England's Jerusalem. During his sojourn in Vienna he soon established contacts with the local party, formed close personal links with one or two individuals and was drawn into the actual business of the Socialist risings. But on the whole his residence abroad brought home to him his Englishness, his dependence on the English milieu, and his preference for English ways. On the day of his return to London, Eileen Power and I met him at the Russell Square Underground and took him out for a meal to a grill room in Southampton Row. Once inside, he eagerly sniffed the air and his face lit up. 'English sausages, how much I missed them in Vienna!' And over a plate of bacon and sausages he told us how much the minutiae of English life meant to him, how conscious he was abroad of being an Englishman and how good it was to be coming home.

At first sight these manifestations of his Englishry may have appeared purely superficial, but in the course of the following two or three years their deeper roots worked their way to the surface. Hugh was a determined and clear-cut anti-Munichite: an attitude which endeared him to Hugh Dalton, but for a time brought him into conflict with Evan Durbin. He moved fast to a belief in the inevitability or indeed the necessity of war with Hitler – a war that would not only rescue the world from a dreadful tyranny, but save the independence and the integrity of England. His attitude was probably more uncompromising than that of any other of the Labour men I knew, except perhaps Hugh Dalton. In the spring of 1939 we all attended a Labour Conference in the Garden House Hotel at Cambridge devoted to a discussion of the international situation. Stafford Cripps, assisted by Konni Zilliacus, urged the socialists to resist the preparations for war. In a speech remarkable for its closely argued *non-sequiturs* Cripps took the line that of the two evils, imperialism and fascism, imperialism was the more abhorrent, and that a successful war against Hitler would, while destroying fascism, strengthen British imperialism. Sentiments like these when uttered by Zilliacus were not of course taken seriously. Coming from Cripps and delivered with the cold ruthlessness of a hanging judge they were bound to shock all of us, even Evan Durbin, very profoundly. After the conference Douglas Jay drove Hugh and some of us to London, and in his crowded car we all studiously avoided all reference to Cripps. It was not until we had got to London that Hugh laughingly and angrily – a characteristic mixture – gave vent to his feelings about Cripps and the coming crisis.

Hugh worked and slaved during the war in MEW and later in the Board of Trade with a concentration, indeed a dedication, which I did not find at all surprising, but he did not expose the springs of his war activity in my company, except once, and once only. One night in early December 1940, during the second or the third of the great night raids on London, German bombs fell on Caroline Place and on two houses in Mecklenburgh Square not far from us. The air-raid wardens told us to get out of the house immediately and would not even give us time to get dressed. So with overcoats over our pyjamas we walked through the air raid to the Lyons Corner House in Coventry Street which at that time stayed open all night. We found it filled with people like ourselves, refugees from bombed or unsafe homes. Some of them slumped drowsily over their cups of tea, others talked and joked with a conspicuous gusto. But of complaints, self-pity, there was not even a suspicion. After listening to these voices for a while Hugh came out with a stream of questions and admissions which revealed more openly than ever before how deeply he felt at that time his involvement with England and her collective future (I hesitate to use the word greatness, for this is not a term Hugh would have used himself). This conversation came back vividly when I read his speech at the 1962 Brighton conference and heard other people's surprised comments on his 'thousand years of English history'.

This brief sketch of the ways Hugh Gaitskell travelled before he entered Parliament cannot do full justice to his whole itinerary. It has left out of account the various by-ways and deviations from his general progress. One of these by-ways must, however, be mentioned here, if only because at certain points it crossed and recrossed his political path. Throughout most of this period Hugh Gaitskell worked and regarded himself as a professional economist. His mathematical equipment was perhaps insufficient for him ever to have attained the very summit of the profession, but he was a very good economist and promised to become an even better one. But what struck me always in Hugh was not the excellence of his economics but its whole-heartedness. He always set great store by economics as an intellectual equipment and by economists as solvers of economic problems. In Hugh's parlance 'the man is an economist' was not merely a description but a commendation. Unfortunately, his growing involvement with political work prevented him from progressing as far and as fast as he would otherwise have done, and his membership of Parliament and his public office stopped his progress altogether. Even then he entered Parliament excellently equipped as an economist. To the end of his days he could understand and handle an economic argument better than anyone else holding high office in this country.

Hugh Gaitskell

Where his interrupted progress showed itself most was in his undimmed admiration for economics and economists, which I suspect reflected his nostalgia for the profession he had to abandon. I also suspect that had he continued his progress as an economist he might also have developed a more sceptical attitude to economic argumentation. I certainly do not know of any truly outstanding economist with the requisite scholarly knowledge of the subject – Samuelson, Hicks, Solow, Arrow, Joan Robinson – who have not seen through the claims of economic theory as a self-sufficient source of economic wisdom. In the thirties Hugh Gaitskell, when challenged – and challenged he frequently was – would be prepared to admit that economics by itself could provide only a limited contribution to the solution of problems, even where problems happened to be mainly economic. Yet he never ceased to approach economic problems as a theoretical economist. He did so in the Ministry of Fuel and Power, in the devaluation crisis of 1949, in the more recent discussions of England's payment problems and again in his attitude to the Common Market. And I have the impression that he listened to economists with far greater respect than to any experts in other fields of social and political inquiry. Whether this was a source of strength or a source of weakness to him in the 1950s and 1960s only those can say who observed him more closely in that period than I could.

I have not written the story of Hugh Gaitskell in the thirties and forties, but merely traced his emergence as a Gaitskellite. I have said very little of Hugh as a friend and a man, gay, affectionate, gentle and generous, yet as unyielding as a rock when it came to principles and loyalties. And I have said nothing at all of Hugh's non-political and non-intellectual pursuits – his acute literary tastes, his exalted view of D. H. Lawrence, his interest in modern painting, or his half-philistine attitudes to music and entertainments. I have left these sides of Hugh out, partly because I could think of one or two persons who could do this much better than I, but mainly because I do not believe this side of Hugh would have made a consecutive story. For it is surprising how little he changed as a man or as a friend through the years in which I knew him. I met him for the last time a week or two before his final illness at an intimate dinner party at the Kaldors' after a meeting of socialist economists in Cambridge, who had gathered to demonstrate to Hugh their support for his stand on the Common Market. He was obviously pleased to find himself on the same side as the economists whose economics he greatly admired, and yet amused that he should now have become a hero to some of the people to whom, in his own words, he had been 'a fascist beast' only a few weeks previously. But to me (we had a few days previously exchanged letters about the Common Market in which we recorded the parting of our ways) it was a nostalgic and a reassuring experience to watch and to hear him speak and react as he might have done at the University College dinner thirty-five years before.

INDEX

Index

Index

Gladstone, W. E., 167
Gneist, Rudolf, 55
Gobineau, Joseph-Arthur de, 3, 10
Gotha Programme, 167
Gottschalk, 7
Gray, John, 169
Gross National Product, 125, 126, 137
Guizot, Joseph-Arthur de, 23, 52

Habakkuk, H. J., 59, 131
Hall, R. (Sir), 95
Hamlet, 151
Hancock, W. K. (Sir), 57
Harrod, R. (Sir), 171
Harvey, William, 8
Hawgood, J., 171
Hay, D., 123 n. 1
Hayek, F. von, 92
Hegel, G. W., 12, 36–7, 48
Hegelian
    dialectic, 148
    theory of history, 38
    tradition, 154, 155, 160
Hellenic society, 152
Herwegh, Georg, 166
Herzen, Alexander, 158
Hicks, J. R. (Sir), *A Theory of Wages*,
    28 n. 1
Hildebrand (Pope Gregory VII), 3
Hildebrand, B., 36
Hindenburg, Field Marshal, 151
Historical
    problems, 25
    relevance, definition of, 51–2
    schools of 19th cent., 30, 58
Histories
    entrepreneurial, 73
    of the War, Civil, 57
Historiography
    economic, 68
    European, 55–6
    modern, 59
    topics of, 50, 58
History
    agrarian, 71; medieval, 53
    antiquarian, 25, 54, 65, 153
    concerned with contemporary problems,
        56
    concreteness of, 62, 63
    dialectical view of, 36–8
    economic, 22–34; American, 59; and eco-
        nomics, 68; and general, 70; 'models'
        in, 121–2; problem-oriented, 103;

topics of, 32, 65, 66, 67, 68, 69–70
    Marxist theory of, 38
    'new economic', 59–60
    problem-oriented, 64
    relevance of, 31
    uniqueness of, 62, 63
Hungary, 167
    medieval, 151

Iceland, 150
India, 88
    agricultural development, 111–18
    investment in, 115–16
    plan for economic growth, 88
Industrialization, 40–1
    in America, 107
    in India, 115, 116
    in Russia, 107
Industrial Revolution, 41, 42, 69, 87, 106,
    109, 131, 169, 175
Industries, new, 132
Industry
    capital-intensive, 116–17
    labour-intensive, 117
    ship-building, 99, 100
Inflation, German, 26
Innovation, 28, 122, 123, 128
    demand for, 130
    investment in, 131–2, 133
Interest, rate of, 28, 81, 131, 132, 133
International Communist League, 166
International trade, theory of, 27–8
'Interpolation', 39–40, 41
Ireland, 167
Irish society, 152
Italy, 122, 127, 128, 133, 138, 139, 148,
    167
Ivan the Terrible, 52

Japan, 111, 117, 122, 127, 128, 129, 150
Jena, 155
Jenks, Leland H., 59
Jesuit missionaries, 9
Jevons, S., 76
Jewish society, 152
Jewkes, J., 92
Johnson, Dr, 1
Johnson, Harry, 94–8
Johnston, Robert E., 125 n. 1
Jurisprudence, philosophies of, 31

Kaldor, N., 80, 85, 95, 98, 172
Kant, I., 9, 11, 12, 13, 48

Index

Index

Index